ANDRÉ
MAUROIS

BY GEORGES LEMAITRE

Professor of Romanic Languages
STANFORD UNIVERSITY

1939

STANFORD UNIVERSITY PRESS
STANFORD UNIVERSITY, CALIFORNIA

LONDON: HUMPHREY MILFORD
OXFORD UNIVERSITY PRESS

STANFORD UNIVERSITY PRESS
STANFORD UNIVERSITY, CALIFORNIA

LONDON: HUMPHREY MILFORD
OXFORD UNIVERSITY PRESS

———

THE BAKER AND TAYLOR COMPANY
55 FIFTH AVENUE, NEW YORK

THE MARUZEN COMPANY
TOKYO, OSAKA, KYOTO, SENDAI

———

To

C. E. FRYER, F.R. Hist. S.
Kingsford Professor of History, McGill University

THIS VOLUME IS DEDICATED
IN FRIENDSHIP AND ESTEEM

PREFACE

ANDRÉ MAUROIS has attained wide recognition as a master in the art of biography and as an authority upon England and the English. He is also acknowledged as a subtle and penetrating novelist. There is, however, an ethic implied in his works which has not received, so far, its due appreciation. Maurois, it is true, does not offer any categorical answer to the besetting issues of modern life. He does not advocate any particular course of action; he merely enjoins an attitude of mind definitely constructive. At a time when both the necessity of a rapid adaptation to a fast-changing world and the need of retaining the most valuable elements of the past appear to all of us as hopelessly contradictory and yet imperiously vital, his profound wisdom may hold a solution to many of our problems—even, in some ways, a prognostication of our future.

Maurois, let us agree, never forces upon us any theoretical resolution of a difficulty. Setting aside the method of a professed moralist, he presents to us simply what a rich and varied experience has taught him, and he brings to us, intelligently and honestly, the results of a lifetime of personal observation and meditation. Because his message is the expression of the development of his personality, it has been found advisable in the sketch here presented of him to review the main factors which have shaped his whole outlook upon existence, to analyze the argument of his works, and to outline the moral and intellectual environment of France which provided the sources of his philosophy.

I feel particularly indebted in the preparation of this essay to Dr. C. E. Fryer, F.R.Hist.S., Kingsford Professor and Head of the Department of History, McGill University. I wish to express here my deepest gratitude to him for his unfailing kindness in providing me with constant encouragement, advice, and help. My sincere thanks are also due to Miss Janet Oswald for her invaluable secretarial services and to Miss Hilda Gifford for many interesting and important suggestions.

I also wish to acknowledge the courtesy of the Librarie Bernard Grasset for kind permission to quote passages from the works of André Maurois, and the courtesy of Messrs. Harper & Brothers for their authorization to translate into English extracts from texts for which they have the exclusive copyright.

GEORGES LEMAITRE

STANFORD UNIVERSITY
July 1939

CONTENTS

ANDRÉ MAUROIS

1

ANDRÉ MAUROIS' LIFE

VERY FEW modern French writers enjoy such wide popularity both at home and abroad as André Maurois. This is perhaps due to the fact that he proclaims a welcome, reassuring message. In these difficult times many people turn to books in the hope of discovering, if not a definite solution of their problems, at least a measure of help and guidance; in most cases they find only further complications, doubts, devastating criticism, over-bold theories, or fanciful hypotheses. In Maurois, however, they find a conformist, belonging to a definite social order—who loves order for its own sake—and who expresses with great intelligence this eminently social spirit.

The family of Herzog—for such is Maurois' real name—came originally from Alsace. After the Franco-Prussian war of 1870–71, the brothers Fraenckel, prosperous cloth manufacturers at Bischwiller, migrated to Normandy in order to remain French, settling eventually in Elbeuf, not very far from Rouen. They were accompanied by their nephew, young Ernest Herzog, who was to be the father of André Maurois. As the modest cloth factory they established in their new

I

place of abode soon became a thriving concern under the name of "Etablissements Fraenckel et Herzog," they were, in spite of their Jewish extraction, readily accepted by the little group of well-to-do manufacturers who made up local "society" in the little town.

The members of this coterie all bore nearly the same moral characteristics, which were, in fact, the characteristics possessed by average French provincial *bourgeois* at the close of the nineteenth century. Love of order, love of discipline, were basic principles in their conception of life. Honesty was a cardinal virtue as well as the key to prosperity among these business people. Their keen sense of the realities of everyday life tended more often than not to develop into common materialism. Yet a certain moral element was not altogether lacking in the group, for its members were united by a feeling of definite solidarity. The tie was naturally strongest among relatives; but even among otherwise unrelated persons there was an almost complete identity of interests, tastes, and prejudices, constituting a very substantial link. In practice this seemed to give to individual members of the set the right to pry into the affairs of all the others. It also created a warm if somewhat stuffy atmosphere of caste intimacy. With stupid and narrow-minded people life in such surroundings would tend to stifle all originality and freedom of spirit; whereas with intelligent and broad-minded persons such an environment might conduce to a well-balanced outlook on life.

Emile-Salomon-Wilhelm Herzog, born on July 26, 1885, was fortunate in finding from the first a well-regulated and peaceful harmony in his home life. However oppressive he may have found the small-town existence in later years, he never actually revolted against it. Throughout his life he retained the definite stamp left upon him by the strong and coherent impressions of a happy childhood. He learned when young to accept and to obey just orders; and he grew to expect due subordination when in later life he acquired authority over others. Among the earliest influences determining his character there was instilled into him the will to do to the best of his ability whatever he might undertake. Thus he developed all the moral traits of an exemplary and law-abiding citizen.

Emile was sent to school at a very early age, attending first the Lycée d'Elbeuf and later the Lycée Corneille in Rouen. He was always a model pupil, taking first place in practically every subject. He has himself told[1] what he felt he owed to each of his teachers. As might be expected from such a pupil, he absorbed from each of them exactly what he was expected to: from Lecaplain, the physics teacher, he learned the first principles of science; from Mouchel and Lelieuvre, both teachers of mathematics, he acquired accuracy and precision of thought; from Texcier, the teacher of French, a sober taste, a hatred of exaggeration, a sound appreciation of classical literature. At the end of this list of completely orthodox and worthy instructors he adds significantly: "To Chartier . . . . I owe everything."[2] Here appears for the first time an element of disturbing interest.

Emile Chartier, who wrote books under the pen name of "Alain," was, for the time being, a teacher of philosophy at the Lycée Corneille. He is little known

[1] A. Maurois, *Rouen*, Nouvelle Revue Française, Paris, 1928, pp. 16–18.
[2] *Ibid.*, p. 18.

outside France, and even there his reputation has not
extended much beyond a small circle of the *élite*; yet
within this circle, and particularly on those who had
him as a teacher, his influence has been enormous.

Chartier was essentially a teacher who by dint of
appropriate, clever, yet simple questioning could make
the most ordinary boy discover the latent originality of
his own mind. His method was in some respects not
very different from that of Socrates. His classes took
the form not of regular, solemn lectures, but of in-
formal and friendly talks on any subject, chosen apparently at random, though always with a more or less
definite purpose in view. In this way he was able to
keep his pupils interested and mentally alert, eventually awakening them to the possibilities of a genuine
intellectual life of their own. Yet the fact was that,
while the boys might be under the impression that they
themselves were elaborating their own personal, original thoughts, more often than not the ideas springing
up in their fertilized minds were only those implanted
by Chartier himself.

Chartier was a man of generous and truly humani-
tarian spirit. He was shocked by the injustices and
abuses that weigh so heavily on the poor; he looked to
socialism to provide a cure for all social and political
evils. However, though in some respects a radical,
Chartier was nevertheless a *bourgeois*—and a *profes-
seur*. Actual revolution he never wanted. In his opinion a better social order could be attained by suitable
legislation, and he hardly ever felt deterred by the
practical difficulties which would have to be faced in
overcoming the resistance of powerful interests or in
keeping within reasonable bounds the desires of the
working class. His unlimited faith in the efficacy of

inspired thinking for the solution of human problems carried him along.

Chartier was not only a philosopher and a political theorist; he was also a lover of art. He had above all the faculty of making literary art a real and living thing to his classes. Balzac and Stendhal were his favorite authors. Among the philosophers Plato, who is as much a poet as a thinker, was his chief delight. Often his young disciples felt inspired to try their hands at literary composition. As a result of his teaching nearly all of them were roused to cultivate a higher sense of artistic beauty and of intellectual attainment than the more pedestrian students of less gifted masters.

Emile Herzog fell under Chartier's spell. The latter's theories of social reform strongly appealed to the sensitive lad. He had heard much talk about labor troubles at home and with his inborn respect for discipline and order was eager to uphold what was right and just. At the same time young Herzog readily discovered within himself strong literary and artistic aspirations, a desire for a colorful, romantic existence, not lacking in higher spiritual aims. For a time he contemplated a university career; and after leaving the Lycée Corneille he received permission from his father to continue his studies at the University of Caen, where he took the degree of Licencié in Philosophy.

The whole course of his studies, largely owing to the influence of Chartier, had aroused in him ideas that were in complete antithesis to those of his early surroundings. The stern and practical-minded manufacturers of his native place could hardly be expected to approve of his magnanimous but rather utopian social theories. The disinterested pursuit of artistic or intellectual attainments was entirely foreign, if not antag-

onistic, to the philistine spirit of Elbeuf. Many young
men in like circumstances nourish similar hopes and
illusions; ordinarily the realities of life soon put an
end to their fantasies. But in Emile Herzog's case the
fact that he had been an exceedingly responsive and
intelligent student and that he had had in Chartier an
exceptionally able master made adjustment to his environment all the more unpalatable. Nevertheless the
cloth factory was waiting for him, and his family was
counting on him. After doing his military service with
the Seventy-fourth Regiment of Infantry in Rouen, he
came back to Elbeuf in 1904 to enter the family business as a partner of his father and his great-uncle, Henri
Fraenckel.

Emile Herzog's experiences in the field of business
were to leave a deep imprint upon his ideas and his
character. There and then he discovered the full meaning of action. Action, as he saw it, was in no way synony-
mous with wild, unexpected adventures. Most of the
time it was rather to be identified with quiet, slow,
patient effort. Only after long and laborious striving
could something new and something real at last be
brought into being. However, this accomplishment he
judged from his experience to be deeply satisfying to
the human soul—probably representing indeed the element of richest value in the whole of human existence.
A feeling of complete self-realization and fulfillment
was the spiritual reward attached to the process of creation even in its humblest forms and its least prepossess-
ing aspects. Such was the conception of life that had
been accepted unquestioningly by all the members of
his family for several generations; it was postulated by
the whole industrial environment at Elbeuf; it was to
be implied by Emile's own preoccupations and exertions

during a period of approximately ten years. Thus did Emile Herzog acquire a deep understanding and a genuine appreciation of action—action for its own sake. Even when, at a much later date, in the course of the development of his literary career, all prospects of practical action had faded out of his life, he retained a whimsical regret for what he still considered his true moral vocation. As he said: "If I did not have a family, ... if I had not settled down, it seems to me that I could have found real happiness as an Intelligence officer in Morocco or as an administrator in Indo-China. I used to enjoy greatly my position as a captain of industry. . . . ."[3]

However—even though the preceding admission is to be regarded as evidence of the deep love of action which was to remain such a typical feature of his personality throughout his life—one may wonder if memory, by one of her most common, deceptive tricks, has not embellished retrospectively his recollections of the years of industrial activity in Elbeuf. Actually his post at the factory does not seem to have been altogether to his liking. More often than not young Herzog could not help finding his work abominably dull. There were business letters to write, orders to be received or to be sent out, accounts to check, debts to collect, petty quarrels to settle—this was what now constituted his life and bounded his horizon. How different from the beautiful and colorful existence he had lately envisaged! Indeed he was not merely a practical man of action. The young poet in him, the potential artist, the budding philosopher, were becoming restive under the burden and fatigue of incessant business routine. Soon they made

[3] A. Maurois, *Fragments d'un Journal de Vacances*, E. Hazan, Paris, 1929, p. 175.

themselves heard, crying out for the wider and brighter horizons of freedom. But stern reality refused to conform to their ideal romantic aspirations.

At first Emile Herzog had tried to put into practice the elevating and generous theories he had brought back from school and college. He was young, and consequently his views were absolute and uncompromising. He was convinced that reform could be brought about by reasoning; but he soon found, to his great disgust, that people are often strongly opposed to change and resentful of any effort toward improvement. His associates and subordinates preferred to follow the beaten path which had been trodden by their predecessors for generations. Sometimes a clash of interests or blind and stupid prejudices would exasperate the relations between masters and men; but whatever the cause, there was always an undercurrent of antagonism and suspicion between the two sides. The full realization of this situation was a heavy blow to the magnanimous socialism of the young man, causing him bitterly to deplore the ruin of many of his fondest dreams. Life was not keeping the promises of brilliant fulfillment which his academic success had led him to anticipate with youthful and trustful assurance.

He fought against his feeling of frustration as well as he could. Occasionally, when he was able to snatch a brief holiday, he would go to Paris in order to keep in touch with the artistic and intellectual movements of the day—or he would cross the Channel to spend a short time in England among the strange Britishers. These interludes were at least more exciting than the life at Elbeuf! At home in Elbeuf he used to read voraciously, generally books of a serious, heavy nature, by writers like Karl Marx or Auguste Comte, taking quantities of notes and building up a reserve of observations and reflections on a wide variety of subjects.

He tried his hand at writing. First he sent contributions to several local papers and to the literary magazine, *L'Effort*, published in Paris. Once—in 1905—he even went the length of placing a series of short stories in the hands of a printer in Rouen. Subsequently, however, he canceled the order for publication, realizing in time that he had not yet reached his maturity.

He found himself then in the throes of a moral conflict, facing the painful dilemma which was to beset him for many years to come, a dilemma destined to leave a deep and abiding mark upon his personality. On the one side he was bound to his work in the factory by family tradition, by a sense of duty, and also by the increasing realization of a satisfaction to be found in "action" itself. But on the other side the kind of "action" which was imposed on him by his circumstances—a series of uninspiring, humdrum tasks—made him feel that his craving for the higher spiritual life was not receiving its due. So, not without anguish, he became aware acutely that all his distinctive originality, with the potentialities that Chartier had revealed to him, was being dangerously overreached and obscured.

Soon a further perplexity of an entirely different order—far more poignant in its nature—came to be added to his former difficulties. In 1910 he took a trip to Switzerland, there making the acquaintance of a young Russian lady, Janine de Szymkievicz. Two years later he married her and brought her to Elbeuf. He was only twenty-seven years old at the time. This was not one of those *mariages de raison,* such as are so often arranged amongst the good *bourgeois* of Elbeuf—in which all the assets of both parties are coldly and carefully weighed one against the other and where similarities of race, religion, social class, also community of interests of the most material nature are often considered as the best guaranties of success in a matrimonial venture; it was romance, with all that the word implies of a lofty ideal, of a deep and devoted attachment, and, it must be added, of endless possibilities of acute suffering.

Mme Emile Herzog was a woman of striking personality, very intellectual and remarkably cultured. She came of an aristocratic family. Part of her education had been received in Switzerland; for the rest, she had lived in England, which gave her the opportunity of studying at Oxford. Undoubtedly she represented a type of woman far more alluring and attractive than the average *bourgeoise* in Elbeuf. Of great importance to Emile Herzog's future career was the fact that his wife brought him into a close acquaintance with English civilization and culture. Already he had some knowledge of England and of the English language. His interest in this direction was now kindled afresh and he was soon to find in English writers an inexhaustible field for his eager study.

Meanwhile Mme Herzog was finding it none too easy to adapt herself to the sleepy French provincial town whose god was *bourgeois* respectability. Attracted as she was by the glamorous side of life, she chafed under the narrow conventional rules prevailing in her new environment. For her, the dull security of Elbeuf and the cloth factory was daily becoming more deadening to the spirit and would soon utterly destroy it.

Of this Emile Herzog was only too well aware. For many years he had been himself dissatisfied with the drab routine imposed on him by his occupation, and he

was longing for a broader, fuller experience. He felt
that he was wasting the best years of his youth and the
even more precious potentialities that perhaps were his.
Nevertheless it was not easy for him to tear himself
away from his moorings. Opposed to his artistic self
there was the other side of his nature, that of the conservative *bourgeois*, firmly attached to family and tradition. To leave the factory would have appeared to
his people and to himself an act of desertion. He considered that the management of the factory was his
duty, and he would do his duty—whatever it was and
however little he might like it.

These difficulties were complicated by even more
delicate problems, such as might be expected to arise
between two young married people of different temperament and outlook in the midst of their first efforts
toward mutual adaptation under trying circumstances.
By way of compromise for the time being, though they
continued to regard the home in Elbeuf as their domi-
cile, the Herzogs rented a small apartment in Paris,
in the Rue Ampère, in order to facilitate more frequent
visits to the capital.

In 1914 war broke out. At first it brought Emile
Herzog release—release from the grip of the problems
which had been harrowing him for several years. Because of his knowledge of English he was attached as
an interpreter to the British Expeditionary Force in
France. For him this held out just the kind of experience he had been more or less unconsciously yearning
for since his adolescent days: a colorful life, with a spice
of danger, with perpetual change and excitement, and
with the unexpected always happening. It was almost
like a dream, in grim yet—it must be said—welcome
contrast to the humdrum existence at Elbeuf. The

trials and troubles of the past seemed temporarily to
have been eclipsed by the tremendous phantasmagoria
of the present.

The most important element of this new experience
of his was, beyond any doubt, a personal and direct acquaintance with the British. He already knew their
language and their literature quite well, but their essential character, as revealed to him in action, was the great
discovery of this period of his life. In 1918, under the
pen name of "André Maurois," he published *Les
Silences du Colonel Bramble*. The book was of rather
a light nature, comprising short stories, anecdotes,
pieces of dialogue, simply but cleverly and humorously
woven together. But it proved an enormous success.
During the years of the war, millions of Britishers had
lived and fought in France, and the French had come
to appreciate these queer, taciturn fellows with a
warmth and sincerity that was not the outcome of official propaganda. Any Frenchman, whether soldier or
civilian, who had been in direct contact with *les Anglais*
had come to regard them with genuine esteem, often
with admiration, though not without the *arrière-pensée*
that they were very funny people. Maurois' book ex-
pressed clearly and intelligently what the average
Frenchman then felt vaguely and confusedly about the
British. The blend of sincere appreciation and amused
but kindly irony that characterizes the book made it so
popular that almost overnight the name of Maurois
became famous throughout France.

Not only did the war provide a breathing spell for
Maurois in the midst of his professional and domestic
difficulties—not only did it offer him a unique opportunity to write a "best-seller" and achieve literary
fame—it brought him a revelation, which was to give

his whole life a definite direction and meaning. One of the disharmonies within his existence at Elbeuf had been the realization that "action" was in his case indissolubly linked with mediocre routine and dullness of thought, all of which his higher self loathed. Now, on coming into direct and close contact with the English, he made the interesting discovery that a perfect blend of practical activity and spiritual attainment could be achieved within the compass of a unified personality. He found the English essentially men of action. At the same time even in their everyday conduct, in their quiet and loyal acceptance of duty, in their unquestioning adherence to a rule once adopted, in their sense of humor even when overwhelmed by adversity, he discovered a source of subtle hidden poetry. It is probable that the unusual and romantic circumstances of his association with the English, in the midst of adventures and dangers, helped greatly in bringing him to a realization of this poetical element in English life. It is even possible that these very circumstances may have led him to overrate that element and to attribute to English people qualities which were to some extent a product of his own imagining. By whatever process this was brought about, it is certain that from that time on the typical Englishman was in his eyes the symbol of a fulfillment for which he himself had been searching in vain. Henceforward the interpretation — his interpretation — of Britain appeared to him to be his great mission in life.

Meanwhile André Maurois' personal problems had come no nearer to a normal and satisfactory solution. When he returned to private life again after the war, he found himself face to face with the old difficulties. As difficulties they were no less sharply defined than they had been in 1914. In some respects they were now even dangerously aggravated. His old manufacturing enterprise in the small town of Elbeuf claimed his attention once more. He had to provide for his family, and to this end the cloth factory was financially an asset that he could hardly afford to throw away. Moreover Maurois still held the same strict conception of his obligations. His father was growing old. Family tradition required him to stick to his post; he did so. But after the excitement of the war he felt the monotony of the humdrum life at Elbeuf more keenly than ever. Action he still enjoyed for its own sake; but labor problems in postwar France were more acute and more bitter than they had ever been. As the head of an industrial concern Maurois was soon wearing himself out in endless petty conflicts; very soon the desire to escape from this drudgery became more urgent than at any time before.

Above all, his sudden and remarkable success as a writer had fostered in him the conviction that he would find on a more intellectual plane a suitable opportunity for achieving his ambitions. The hope of making a brilliant literary career was now rapidly growing within him, keeping pace with the longing for a freer and richer expression of his higher personality. But was a literary vocation compatible with cloth manufacturing in Elbeuf? Was not Paris the only place that could offer the perfect environment for creative work? Should he not abandon Elbeuf for the capital? Then other influences were also coming into play. During the war the home at Elbeuf had been, as a matter of course, broken up. Years of separation and absence had not helped to overcome certain divergencies in temperament and outlook. Maurois could understand how life played havoc with romance.

When the question of reorganizing the family life came to be discussed, Maurois decided upon a twofold division of his time and interests, as before the war. But the altered balance of the two sides shows the direction things were taking. Part of the year—usually a few months in the summer—he spent at La Saussaye, within easy access of the factory. The rest of his time was given to Paris. Here he rented a large flat in the residential suburb of Neuilly. Yet, well-mannered provincial that he was, he could not help but shrink occasionally from the people he met in the literary groups of the capital. The aggressive, artificial, and frivolous qualities displayed by many of them were highly repellent to his polished, sincere, and thoughtful nature. In the course of time he became accustomed to it all; yet the first contact with this society was not altogether pleasant, and many of his experiences only added to his uneasiness and uncertainty.

In writing he found an outlet for his troubled feelings. It is noteworthy that Maurois in his works during this period did not give expression to the problems and difficulties besetting him at the time. Such burning issues he probably could not treat immediately as subject matter for literature. The source of the principal strains to be found in the books he published then may be traced to the earlier phase of his life—the period extending from the time he began business up to the termination of the war. In these works one finds the bold and generous spirit which he had cultivated in his early twenties: a romantic conception of life, a rather poetical representation of the English, a fervent predilection for creative activity.

In *Ni Ange, ni Bête* (1919), his next work, Maurois combined some of his own past impressions with the adventures of a young engineer who actually lived in the idealistic atmosphere of 1848. In this story the vain efforts of a young man to apply his magnanimous but impracticable theories to stern reality and the troubles and difficulties that arise between himself and his young wife were presented, not wholly sympathetically, as if by a witness having no patience with the hero's pedantic idealism. The book was almost a failure. *Les Discours du Docteur O'Grady* (1922) fared little better. The bulk of this work, written in the same vein as *Les Silences du Colonel Bramble*, had been composed a few years before[4] but was now published at a time when the personal antagonism between Poincaré and Lloyd George had converted Franco-British relations into a sort of diplomatic boxing match. Maurois perhaps hoped that his book would help to clear the atmosphere. As a matter of fact, it went almost unnoticed. Shortly afterward *Ariel* appeared. This biography of Shelley was written in exactly the same spirit as *Ni Ange, ni Bête*. Maurois' aim was to show the clash between vulgar, disappointing reality and the idealism of a noble-hearted man—the difficulties that he meets with when he tries to put his ideals into practice and the sentimental complications that inevitably ensue. Maurois himself had gone through very similar experiences, and he was feeling profoundly dissatisfied with the way in which he had treated his own problems. He was therefore inclined to view the efforts of his hero with scepticism—even to vent his sarcasm upon them. Yet, permeated as it is throughout with

---

[4] *Les Discours du Docteur O'Grady* had already appeared in 1918 in a somewhat different form, under the title of *Le Général Bramble;* the latter was a de luxe edition, and only a limited number of copies were printed.

the personality of Shelley, the book has a deep and compelling charm. With the publication of *Ariel* (1923), Maurois began to be counted among the greater French writers.

France was just then passing through a period of political anxiety and restlessness. In 1923 the military occupation of the Ruhr had ushered in an era of bold adventure in home and foreign politics. Inflation became almost an established system. French ministries were made and unmade even more rapidly than usual. In the prevailing uncertainty, *Plutarque a menti*, a book by J. de Pierrefeu, containing disturbing revelations about several of the most distinguished French war-time leaders, swept the whole country—a serious symptom of the general uneasiness, lack of confidence, and even positive discontent. At this juncture, and in reply to *Plutarque a menti*, Maurois issued an appeal for discipline in his volume, *Dialogues sur le Commandement* (1924). This little book did not simply offer a philosophy of action: it was "action" itself. It represented Maurois' personal contribution to a nation-wide movement toward a revival of sound and responsible citizenship, a movement which eventually restored, temporarily at least, some measure of political balance in the country.

Meanwhile, Maurois' own problems were now rapidly approaching a climax. The time had come when he had to choose definitely between Elbeuf and Paris. Was he to be essentially a businessman, cultivating literature as a hobby, or a professional writer, making a living with his pen? On the one hand, the artist in him was loath to remain buried any longer in the drab environment of a little provincial town. On the other hand, the conformist *bourgeois* part of him felt reluctant to sever definitely the ties of family tradition. The complexity of the situation was heightened by the fact that on both sides other persons were deeply involved in the problem. The main obstacles to a solution disappeared when the chief protagonists of Maurois' moral drama, his wife and his father, passed away; his wife died in 1924, his father in 1925.

Soon afterward Maurois left Elbeuf for good and settled in Paris with the definite intention of being a writer and nothing else. Then he married again. His second wife, Simone de Caillavet, was the granddaughter of Mme Arman de Caillavet, famous as the friend of Anatole France. She moved in one of the most cultivated and refined circles in Paris, while she was herself eminently well-balanced and stable. In her Maurois found, allied to great personal distinction and charm, all the virtues that a conservative Frenchman feels he is entitled to expect in his wife. Thus, in his early forties, Maurois succeeded in solving at last his two fundamental difficulties—that of his profession and that of his home life. The solutions he adopted could not but involve certain serious sacrifices. However, his losses were offset by very substantial compensations. He felt free at present to follow the calling of his choice: his great literary success had made him financially independent, and justified morally the discarding of the business traditions of his family. Moreover he was to find in his new home the qualities that make for domestic happiness.

Nevertheless a state of perfect equilibrium was not attained in a day. Adaptation was again necessary. The man who had undergone so many moral vicissitudes could not adjust himself all at once to sudden tranquillity. Gusts of feeling out of the past would sweep over him unexpectedly and stir him to his very depths. The peaceful family life for which he had yearned in times of stress seemed to him in realization almost too calm. The element of restlessness was in him still.

Between 1925 and 1930 Maurois went through a period of exceptionally intense and rich literary productivity. As in the past, literature once more provided a channel for his thwarted aspirations and feelings. So he found an outlet for the obsessions of the past and could rid himself, as it were, of all possible sources of moral disturbance. The topics of his new books no longer related to the earliest stages of a young man's experience. They now concerned the crucial issues which had lain at the core of his destiny as a man, which had stirred his whole being to its very depths, and for which, as now appeared to him, he had found only an approximate answer. So his books, while helping to relieve him from dangerous recollections and moral strain, at the same time were enriched by all the deep emotions he had experienced through years of tribulation and trial.

In rapid succession appeared his masterpieces: *Bernard Quesnay* (1926), *La Vie de Disraëli* (1927), *Climats* (1928), and *Don Juan ou la Vie de Byron* (1930). The connection between the general subject of each of these works and Maurois' own life problems is easily discernible. In *Bernard Quesnay* he considered the puzzling dilemma involved in a choice between a dull, drab, dutiful life and an interesting, brilliant, carefree existence. The *Vie de Disraëli* was a study of action not confined to a mediocre routine but bringing forth magnificent results. In *Climats* the mutual reactions of husband and wife—or rather of a husband and two successive wives, one frivolous, one serious—were presented in most intimate detail. In *Byron*, Maurois weighed the dangers that are to be encountered when all troublesome social conventions are deliberately cast aside.

After thus unburdening himself vicariously, as it were, of his own psychological past, Maurois' course became smoother. The English influences contributing to this process of stabilization cannot be overemphasized. England provided Maurois with a much-needed ideal, compensating him for his personal disappointments and losses. English history and literature offered a field of intellectual activity which enabled him to display his own creative faculties to their best advantage, and literary creation was in his case a powerful element of self-realization and satisfaction. Moreover, in his contact with English civilization and culture—sound and solid to the core—Maurois doubtless absorbed something of the fundamental wisdom and steadiness of the English people.

By degrees the warm atmosphere of home and the bringing up of a young family brought him contentment and peace. Time and the passing years also were not without their influence in that respect. Philippe Marcenat, a character in one of Maurois' books, who expresses many of Maurois' individual views and even seems to represent to a large extent the person of the author himself, explains in the following manner his growing tranquillity in like circumstances: "I feel I am entering a calmer zone. You remember . . . . I used to compare my life to a symphony wherein mingled several themes: the theme of the Knight, the theme of the cynic, the theme of the rival. I still hear them, even quite strongly. But I also hear in the orchestra one particular instrument—I don't know which it is—repeating with soft, firm tones a theme made of a few notes, tender and soothing. It is the theme of serenity; it resembles the theme of old age."[5]

In this process of moral stabilization, Madame André Maurois has played a truly outstanding part. Endowed as she was with a sensitive, vibrant soul, she came to conceive it her aim and purpose in life to devote herself entirely to the person and to the artistic creations of her husband. Indeed she succeeded in identifying herself almost completely with his work. Thanks to her remarkable intellectual gifts—though shunning for herself the glare of indiscreet publicity—she fostered through constant, trusted collaboration the most accomplished literary achievements of André Maurois himself.

In recent years, Maurois' life, outwardly eventful and brilliant, became deeply satisfying and calm. His headquarters remained in Paris, his permanent residence being still at Neuilly, close by the famous Bois de Boulogne. During the summer he often went to the country estate of Essendieras in the old province of Périgord. Thanks to his universally recognized eminence as a writer, to his personal charm and to his consummate tact, he played an important part in the literary life of the capital. He was very much sought after for public lectures, for important committees, and for official and fashionable functions. Among his personal friends are such outstanding men as André Gide, Paul Morand, Paul Valéry, and François Mauriac. He himself is one of the very few modern French writers who enjoy the favor of a large reading public as well as the appreciation of an *élite* of critics and connoisseurs.

Such a complete and rapid success could not but pro-

[5] A. Maurois, *Climats*, Grasset, Paris, 1928, p. 277.

voke resentment in certain quarters. In 1928, a young Egyptian, Hadji Vassilios, writing under the pen-name of "Auriant," published in the *Mercure de France* a virulent and abusive article hurling at Maurois the direct and open accusation of plagiarism.[6] He declared that Maurois' *Vie de Shelley* was imitated from Dr. Dowden's book on the same subject, further that his *Vie de Disraëli* followed too closely Monypenny and Buckle's *Life of Benjamin Disraeli*. Even though this accusation lacked foundation in fact, Maurois took the trouble to reply.[7] He showed that he had indeed used—among others— the sources mentioned by Auriant, but that he had taken from them well-known facts, and not viewpoints or turns of expression which might be considered as the property of a particular writer. This reply attracted fresh accusations,[8] which Maurois did not leave unanswered.[9]

Meanwhile, other parties had been drawn into the controversy. Thus Frank Harris stepped in to affirm that sections of Maurois' essay on Oscar Wilde (in *Etudes Anglaises*) had been taken from his own book, *Oscar Wilde, His Life and Confessions*. On the other hand, Sir Edmund Gosse in a letter testified to the complete genuineness and originality of Maurois' writings.[10] Further opinions were called forth on both sides. Gradually, however, the excitement subsided and eventually the

[6] Auriant, "Un Ecrivain Original. M. André Maurois," *Mercure de France*, Vol. CCII, No. 713, March 1, 1928, pp. 298–323.

[7] A. Maurois, "Une Lettre," *Mercure de France*, Vol. CCII, No. 715, April 1, 1928, pp. 55–73.

[8] Auriant, "Un Ecrivain Original. M. André Maurois (Suite)," *ibid.*, Vol. CCIII, No. 716, April 15, 1928, pp. 452–72.

[9] "Une Lettre de M. André Maurois," *ibid.*, Vol. CCIII, No. 717, May 1, 1928, pp. 716–19.

[10] Sir Edmund Gosse's letter is quoted in "Une Lettre de M. André Maurois," *ibid.*, Vol. CCIII, No. 717, May 1, 1928, p. 718.

consensus of the most fair-minded critics was that in no case had Maurois' methods of documentation violated the strictest rules of literary ethics.

This controversy, however untoward and unpleasantly sensational it may have been, failed to damage Maurois' reputation either at home or abroad. In 1938 Maurois was elected to the French Academy. In England, whither he frequently repairs, he now possesses innumerable admirers and friends. He was well acquainted with Rudyard Kipling. He is even said to be honored by the gracious recognition of King George VI. His talent as an academic lecturer made him welcome at Cambridge, where in 1928 he gave at Trinity College, under the Clarke Foundation, a course on "Aspects of Biography." In France he has come to be accepted as an expert and authority on all things English; he is a strong advocate of Franco-British friendship and is sometimes referred to, humorously but not without point, as a "spiritual *Tunnel sous la Manche.*" Tirelessly he pursues his mission and task of interpreting the English, past and present, to the French. His book *Les Anglais,* his *Etudes Anglaises,* further, his *Le Côté de Chelsea, Edouard VII et son temps,* and *Magiciens et Logiciens,* and finally his *Histoire d'Angleterre* are documents of considerable informative value to the large section of the French public interested in the multifarious aspects of England.

Besides England, which after France he will always consider as his second spiritual home, Maurois has lately discovered an entirely new field of interest. In 1927, in the course of a lecture tour in the United States, he had his first direct experience of the newer— and at that time prosperous—civilization of America. He was so impressed with the spectacle that when he received an invitation to come and teach for a few months at Princeton University in 1930 he eagerly accepted this opportunity to secure a closer acquaintance with the New World. In 1933 a Doctor's degree *honoris causa* was conferred on him by Princeton; in 1936 and also in 1939 he again made the trip across the Atlantic, obviously prompted by a growing sympathy for and interest in things American.

America and the American people, however, could not play in Maurois' life a part in any way comparable to that filled a few years before by England and the English. He was older now—the cast of his mind was practically determined and fixed—and his time was far too limited in view of the vastness and complexity of his new subject of study. To be sure, in the course of his visits to the United States he became quite well acquainted with American university life; but outside this very definite environment the information he gathered was of rather a general nature. Three books—*Contact, L'Amérique Inattendue,* and *Chantiers Américains*—brought France the results of Maurois' observations and enquiries, all of them very clever without a doubt, but lacking the intuitive quality of revelation and the personal accent of his very first sketches of England.

Indeed most of the recent works of Maurois—those which have appeared since 1930 approximately—lack the personal accent, the fire and power of his earlier literary creations. The fundamental cause of the change is probably that Maurois' own life—now completely smooth, harmonious—no longer provides him with a store of thwarted and suppressed aspirations such as had gone to enrich his masterpieces. He must now have recourse to external observation and description mainly. All his latest novels—*Le Peseur d'Ames* (1931), *Le*

Cercle de Famille (1932), *L'Instinct du Bonheur*
(1934), *La Machine à Lire les Pensées* (1937)—bear
the marks of clever and objective but at the same time
somewhat abstract and theoretical ingenuity.

The most remarkable feature of Maurois' late intellectual evolution is the co-ordination of his thoughts
and ideas into a coherent philosophy. As a result of his
early association with Chartier, Maurois has ever been
prone to philosophize. In the reflective mood of matur-
ing age he now systematically takes stock of what life
has brought him and of all that it has taught him. In
three collections of essays—*Mes Songes que voici, Sentiments et Coutumes,* and *Un Art de Vivre*—he sum-
marizes the essentials of his findings in these respects.
More generally in all his recent writings—whether in
the field of history, of criticism, or of fiction—a vigorous original conception of human existence is ex-
pressed or implied.

2

THE ENGLISH PEOPLE
AS SEEN BY MAUROIS

TO THE average Frenchman, Maurois is of all contemporary French writers the one who knows most about *les Anglais*. He is in France the recognized authority on English literature, English customs, and English society. Indeed, when a well-known Parisian publisher decided to present to the public a series of studies of women of different nationalities, he naturally counted on Maurois to write about Englishwomen—much to Maurois' embarrassment: Maurois protested modestly that he had no special knowledge of the subject.[1]

In point of fact his experience does not by any means cover all the representative types of Briton. During the war he became acquainted with officers of various British regiments. After the war he was received in the literary and artistic circles of English society. But the merchant, the farmer, the sailor, the workingman, each of whom has an important place in English life, seem to have remained outside the range of his direct observation. Thus the picture that he draws of the British people is far from applying to all sections of that great community. Nevertheless, the small groups he depicts

---

[1] A. Maurois, *L'Anglaise et d'autres femmes*, Nouvelle Société d'Éditions, Paris, 1932, p. 9.

represent those elements that have contributed most to Britain's greatness, and therefore their portrayal is of engrossing interest.

In his book, *Les Anglais,* and in the short pamphlet, *Conseils à un jeune Français partant pour l'Angleterre,* Maurois presents concisely a few generalizations and conclusions regarding the British. But *Les Silences du Colonel Bramble* and *Les Discours du Docteur O'Grady* offer the most striking and also the most entertaining picture of English character in an original and colorful setting. Both volumes are based on Maurois' recollections of his war-time experiences with the British Army in the capacity of interpreter. Maurois himself appears in the two books, though always unobtrusively, under the transparent disguise of the interpreter, Aurelle.

The personal views of the author on life and mankind find their way into the more or less philosophical dialogues which are represented as being carried on by sundry officers around the mess-table. These conversations are not the least of the books' attractions. They are clever, witty, lively, sometimes even brilliant—perhaps indeed more so than might reasonably be expected in such circumstances and of such people. Dangerous topics, like morals and religion, are often broached, and bold and daring discussions occasionally are started; but if such are likely to prove awkward, Colonel Bramble hastily sets the gramophone playing. The war itself provides a colorful background, with its ever recurring themes of slaughter and sex. Heroism also is touched upon, sometimes explained by stupidity but always relieved by humor. Above all, danger reveals characters in their true light and several personalities gradually take shape before our eyes. Their individual queer attitudes and moods are shown up very distinctly, but at the same time we perceive the powerful and impressive unity of spirit that binds them all together.

Major Parker is perhaps the most typically English of them all. Moderate and sensible, broad-minded—without being lax—he is a man of sound principle. He is cultured, but makes no display of his accomplishments. He reads Xenophon, not to show how scholarly he is but obviously because it is his hobby. Dr. O'Grady is an Irishman—almost a caricature of the typical Irishman—whimsical, talkative and witty, artistic and imaginative, audacious in his theories, idealistic and cynical by turns. He may be at times a little lacking in common sense, but this is hardly noticeable amidst the dazzling fireworks of his conversation. Colonel Bramble hails from Scotland. He does not talk much; when he is deeply moved, he merely grunts inarticulately "Och!" Yet behind his rugged appearance one is aware of a true and kindly soul, capable of warm human feeling. Lieutenant Dundas is the unsophisticated British lad, with pink cheeks, an athletic body, and a clean mind, but not a single idea in his head. A thoroughly likable boy! Asked what he would do if a revolution broke out, he answered simply, *"Je me ferais secrétaire d'un club de golf."*[2]

From Maurois' account of their actions, reactions, talk, and mannerisms there gradually forms in the reader's mind a complex and yet definite impression of the thousand trifling or important idiosyncrasies which go to make the English absolutely different from all other nations—and especially from the French. Indeed, the portrayal of the English by Maurois is

---

[2] A. Maurois, *Les Discours du Docteur O'Grady*, Grasset, Paris, 1922, p. 175.

almost always made by a comparison with the French. This method is perfectly justifiable in a work intended for French readers, possessing as it does the simplicity and evocative power of a sculptured frieze in relief against a background of different and often discreetly contrasting color.

In the English the feature which seems the most disconcerting to a cultured Frenchman is perhaps the apparent contrast between their intellectual achievements and their attitude toward moral and practical affairs. On the one hand, their wonderful literature, their discoveries in the field of science, and their contributions to philosophy indisputably bear witness to their keen intelligence. On the other hand, when confronted with a seemingly simple question of conduct or policy, to which there appears to be but one rational answer, the English do not feel bound by those exigencies of logic which control so strictly the mind of the French. In his own mind a Frenchman will pursue nimbly, and with evident delight to himself, a clear, unimpeachable, dialectical argumentation; he will find in it compelling, nay irresistible, motivation for his behavior. Intellectual dialectic appeals to the Englishman but slightly and does not in any way condition his attitude toward reality. In fact he will become reticent and suspicious if a solution propounded to him is too compellingly logical. Maurois recalls how once at Geneva the French delegates proposed what seemed to them a perfectly simple and rational plan for European disarmament. The English rejected it *because* it was too clear and *therefore*, they felt, "it couldn't work."[8] So Maurois gives the French the following advice con-

[8] A. Maurois, *Conseils à un jeune Français partant pour l'Angleterre*, Les Amis d'Edouard, Paris, 1927, p. 12.

cerning the English: "When you want to convince them, don't reason too clearly. You French are apt to think that you have gained your point when you have demonstrated to them that you are right. To them it is immaterial whether logic proves them to be right or wrong. On the contrary, they rather distrust an argument that is too well reasoned."[4]

The worship of reason, of cleverness, which is so typical of France, has absolutely no counterpart in England. English people do not hold that reason is the rule and measure of the universe. As Maurois shows, there is a wealth of revelation in regard to the different mentalities of the two nations in the humorous criticism leveled against France by an Englishman, who said that France is a country "where 2 and 2 are *always* 4."[5] Individual cleverness is not held in any high esteem by the British and may even rouse their suspicions. In their view the remark, " 'He is clever,' always implies a shade of disapproval or distrust."[6] Toward books, they often show hardly more than a contemptuous and condescending tolerance. "You are entering the only country where a man will say frankly to a writer: 'Books? I have never read a single one. . . . . When I try to, I realize that I don't remember a word of what I've read. . . . . What's the use of trying then?' Besides, the English leave you free to read and they make fun of you a little for it, as they would make fun of a collector of rhinoceros horns. But they would better understand the taste for rhinoceros."[7]

For lack of a vigorous, critical rationalism, the most

---

[4] *Conseils à un jeune Français*, pp. 11–12.

[5] A. Maurois, *Les Anglais*, Flammarion, Paris, 1935, p. 24.

[6] *Ibid.*, p. 24.

[7] *Conseils à un jeune Français*, pp. 8–9.

fantastic beliefs arise and flourish in profusion. Maurois is astonished and also amused to note[8] that stories of ghosts, haunted houses, second sight—such as would elicit only a skeptical smile from a logical-minded Frenchman—are almost universally and unquestioningly accepted by these Islanders. There superstitions are upheld by otherwise sensible and intelligent persons: Colonel Bramble would never dare to light three cigarettes with one match;[9] and Parker—the sane and sensible Parker—salutes the magpies.[10]

Maurois kindly tries to explain[11] this English trait of character as due to the influence of the climate of the country. Indeed the fog which in England so often envelops the landscape with a phantasmagoric atmosphere, blurring clear outlines, may have fostered hallucinations and a sense of the mysterious, the irrational, and the supernatural. But what of the nonsense literature which delights the hearts of so many English people of all ages? The *Nonsense Rhymes* of Edward Lear fill an Englishman with glee—a Frenchman with nothing but stupefaction.[12] As a matter of fact, an Englishman derives an innocent enjoyment from a playful and fanciful juggling with solemn ideas. The Frenchman, who respects ideas, fails to see the point— as there generally is no point—and is "not amused"; he is even likely to be thoroughly exasperated. The fantastic, utterly impossible adventures of Alice in Wonderland are dear to the heart of every English reader. Even French children, on hearing such tales, would

[8] A. Maurois, *Les Silences du Colonel Bramble*, Grasset, Paris, 1921, pp. 146–47.

[9] *Ibid.*, p. 205.

[10] *Les Discours du Docteur O'Grady*, p. 171.

[11] *Les Anglais*, p. 13. [12] *Ibid.*, p. 24.

deçlare spontaneously—as did the six-year-old daughter of Interpreter Aurelle: *"C'est trop stupide."*[13]

Far from blushing for their lack of intellectualism, many Englishmen would pride themselves, though perhaps somewhat humorously, on the extent of their stupidity: " 'We are stupid,' repeated Major Parker vigorously . . . . 'and it is a great strength. When we happen to be in danger, we do not realize it, because we are little given to reflection; so we remain calm and we pull through almost always with honour.'—'Always,' corrected Colonel Bramble."[14]

Yet Maurois is not content with such a one-sided and obviously incomplete explanation of the complex problem of the Britishers' mentality, for he remarks: "It is a very silly mistake to think them less clever than we are, however much my friend Major Parker may seem to enjoy saying so. The truth is that their minds work along lines different from ours."[15]

In order to draw a challenging picture of the ways of thought that in his judgment are peculiarly English, Maurois employs a musical comparison[16] taken from the prelude to Wagner's *Das Rheingold*. In this, a deep, monotonous, resounding harmony, symbolizing musically the passage of Time—as well as the flow of the River Rhine—murmurs through the whole prelude in slow, powerful, mysterious waves. Almost unconsciously, yet irresistibly, the listener is carried away on a strong, undulating current, quiet, calm, and overpowering. From time to time the sound of some isolated instrument, generally a violin, will be heard

---

[13] *Les Discours du Docteur O'Grady*, p. 159.
[14] *Les Silences du Colonel Bramble*, p. 17.
[15] *Ibid.*, pp. 46–47.   [16] *Les Anglais*, p. 29.

above this regular, flowing murmur, sketching a rapid, light, melodious motif. Each of these motifs, figurative of things of beauty, of subtle imaginings, of fantastic dreams, suggests an ephemeral and graceful tracery of intricate pattern against the darker background of depths that are eternal, immense, unfathomable. They are rarely taken up and repeated by the whole orchestra, but soon vanish, one after another, submerged, as it were, in the continuous stream of sound which rolls majestically onward.

This, Maurois considers, may be taken as an image of the mental life of the English nation. In this life the essential is a current of profound feelings, obscure instincts, and automatic reflexes instilled by education—all of them often half-conscious, but powerful and running deep, because they are almost elemental and thoroughly genuine. They constitute truly the basic features of the Englishman's character; they govern his attitude toward life; they determine his actions. The intellect from time to time will surge up to the surface, it is true, yet without fundamentally altering the stream of his sentiments; then, as if in play, it will execute delicate, complicated arabesques, often of striking ingenuity—though unrelated to any control over his practical or moral behavior.

This dualism, dividing the English character into two separate and almost independent domains, carries with it most important consequences. While in France—where reason and action are always closely associated—ideas are regarded as significant and powerful; in England, on the contrary, they are considered merely as anodynes and hardly worthy of serious attention. Thus a George Bernard Shaw can ridicule his English people with sarcasms such as the French would never put up with if leveled at their nation. The English will pay to listen to the sallies made by the witty Irishman at their expense; his criticisms leave them quite unperturbed—they are merely entertained by them. "With us," Maurois says of the French, "ideas are active and dangerous forces, which have to be handled with care. Among the English, actions are so carefully determined by a rigid education that the verbal clowning of a Shaw remains harmless acrobatics, in which the most thorough-going conservative may find amusement without detriment to his conscience. Dr. O'Grady at mess can venture upon the worst blasphemies without perturbing the General or the Padre."[17]

Hence among the British, intellectual activity seems to be relegated to a secondary and somewhat derogatory position. This explains the attitude of many of them toward intellectual problems. "I don't think," says Maurois, "that you can even imagine the contempt in which every form of literary culture is held by a certain type of Englishman."[18] This also accounts for their acceptance, nay their enjoyment, of "nonsense," which is anathema to the French.

But strangely enough, independent thinking gains in quality and strength in proportion to its loss in respect and prestige. "These are only ideas; nothing dangerous there,"[19] seems to be a fundamental viewpoint among the English. The dissociation between actions and ideas enables the English to permit a degree of freedom in the development of the latter that nations more readily guided and swayed by the power of

---

[17] *Les Discours du Docteur O'Grady*, p. 159.
[18] *Conseils à un jeune Français*, p. 8.
[19] *Les Anglais*, p. 24.

reasoning could not grant without the risk of complete internal disruption. If freedom of thought and freedom of speech have been obtained much earlier in Britain than anywhere else on the Continent—if they still prevail there more definitely perhaps than anywhere else in the world—it is mainly because the English realize that for them the exercise of that freedom is without marked consequences and therefore entails no marked inconvenience.

There is another side to this problem besides the political. Pure thought—dissociated from action—has acquired in England a quality all its own. Unfettered by the necessities of practical application, it has attained a spirituality that is outside the experience of the more realistically minded French nation. The grace, the fragrance, the charm of English poetry and its power of evoking images that are *"légères, aériennes, irré elles,"*[20] are, probably for that reason, unmatched in all European literature. Further, as its flexibility is unhampered by logical categories such as those which so strictly and rigidly govern the French mind, pure thought among the English has become an extremely supple and pliable instrument, at once delicate, sharp, and penetrating, and prepared for the most daring and complicated operations. In every respect, it can be said that in England "the divorce between practical life and abstract thought is so complete that thought enjoys absolute liberty."[21]

It may seem, at first sight, rather paradoxical to assign to feelings and sentiments a position of such overwhelming importance in the moral life of the

---

[20] *Les Discours du Docteur O'Grady*, p. 158.
[21] *Ibid.*, p. 160.

English people. Are not the English rated by almost universal consensus as a cold and calculating nation? Maurois, however, does not hesitate to affirm that "at bottom, John Bull is terribly sentimental."[22]

He even goes so far as to say that the British experience emotions of a much deeper and more violent nature than other apparently more temperamental and more demonstrative people. As a matter of fact, this emotional intensity is carefully concealed ordinarily under a calm and composed exterior, and manifests itself outwardly only on rare and special occasions. Then some word or some unusual expression may betray the fire that is smouldering underneath the cool and unruffled surface; more rarely still a sudden conflagration may flare into the open to startle and amaze the unsuspecting onlooker. "Even in the most austere of them one may witness outbreaks of sadism, which, occurring in their well-regulated souls, cause as much surprise as would the appearance of a wild beast on the grass of Hyde Park. When the General, after listening to his beloved Mrs. Finzi-Magrini on the gramophone, gets very red in the face and exclaims in muffled tones, 'Oh! I'd like to bite her neck,' do you imagine he is joking? If you do, you are mistaken. You French people allow some of your newspapers to reproduce voluptuous pictures because you are in fact lacking in temperament. The English forbid such things because they are inclined to dwell upon them with a gloomy intensity."[23]

Among the profound and irrational instincts dwelling in the inmost recesses of the English soul Maurois

---

[22] *Les Silences du Colonel Bramble*, p. 80.
[23] *Les Discours du Docteur O'Grady*, pp. 35–36.

discerns an almost childlike need to believe that everything is—or will be—for the best, an instinctive refusal to see, or to accept as final, the sordidness of life, the crudeness or ugliness of reality. According to Maurois this betokens, on the part of the Englishman, a deep and genuine kindness of heart, a fundamental though somewhat naïve goodness. The Frenchman will look at facts as they are in all their hardness and immorality and will face them clear-sightedly and unflinchingly; the Englishman will show no less bravery under the circumstances, but he requires to be convinced at the same time that every difficulty and adversity will somehow or other issue in a moral good.

On the surface this attitude seems hardly consistent with a sophisticated view of the world; it is more akin to the innocence, confidence, and naiveté of youth. Indeed, the English often give foreigners the impression that they never quite reach mature, sensible, adult comprehension. "You know . . . . the story of Peter Pan, the little boy who never grew up? The English nation is Peter Pan."[24] Their appearance, their pleasures also, are not unlike those of children. "Yes, these admirable men are in certain respects still children. They have retained the pink complexion of children, their deep love of games, and our rustic dugout very often appears to me to house a nurseryful of heroes."[25]

This candid, and seemingly absurd, moral idealism is often regarded by foreigners as a hypocritical cloak covering the most selfish purposes. Not at all, says Maurois: *"L'idéalisme Anglo-Saxon n'est pas hypocrite; il est sincère."*[26] As a matter of fact, the English-

---

[24] *Les Silences du Colonel Bramble*, p. 146.   [25] *Ibid.*, p. 45.
[26] *Les Discours du Docteur O'Grady*, p. 251.

man, like most human beings, generally pursues his own interests and personal desires. But while a "cynical" Frenchman will ordinarily admit to himself at least, and sometimes openly recognize, the true nature of his own aspirations, the Englishman likes to believe that his actions are based on moral grounds alone. So Ruskin could not with a good conscience admire pretty girls unless he repeated to himself that pretty girls are angels.[27] Gladstone persuaded himself, just as easily, that his own decisions coincided with the Divine Will.[28] The Frenchman, a born rationalist, likes to think that all he does is logical, and he is unhappy if he cannot find a link of some sort between logic and his own action. The Englishman would suffer no less acutely if he were unable to discover some agreement between morality and his own purpose. Hence—though often at the cost of a strain on his imagination, but with complete sincerity—he invariably finds a way of convincing himself that his actions or desires are pure and good. In politics "in order to get an Englishman to do something, you must lay before him a plan of action which is consonant with the interests of his country and which could be described, with more or less subtlety, as a moral action."[29]

But however strong may be his power of idealistic and moralizing self-delusion, the Englishman cannot overlook evil altogether. When evil is staring him in the face, so that he can no longer ignore it, he will try to render it harmless, to neutralize it, as it were, in a most singular and original fashion—with the curious weapon of humor. Humor, according to Maurois,[30] is

---

[27] *Les Anglais,* p. 27.   [28] *Ibid.,* p. 27.   [29] *Ibid.,* p. 27.
[30] A. Maurois, *Études Anglaises,* Grasset, Paris, 1927, pp. 142–43.

simply a means of defense against the unpleasant facts
of life which are too obvious and too gross to be either
ignored or interpreted with magnanimity. When confronted with evil, in some form or other—physical,
social, or moral—the Englishman first examines it very
closely. His report upon it may seem dull and insipid
to the unsuspecting, though a plain, matter of fact account of the subject is desirable in order to convey the
impression of an exact and truthful representation of
the evil as it actually appears. Then, by very slight
exaggeration of a detail, the whole picture is shown to
be unreal, to be nothing but a joke; and at the same
time the original evil, with which the picture was so
closely identified, appears also to be unreal and becomes
a joke. The whole point of English humor is to distort
one feature of a situation so slightly that the likeness
of the picture remains convincing and yet sufficiently
to transport both the picture and its subject into the
realm of the ludicrous, where they will seem fantastic
and harmless. A great deal of refinement of a purely
intuitive nature is necessary, in both the teller and the
listener, since too great emphasis of any point would
overreach the mark, just as understatement would fall
short of it. This calls for a form of tact which puzzles
even the cleverest foreigners—especially those who do
not continually keep in mind the typically English
tendency to ward off evil and subtly turn it into something that can harm no one.

When, for one reason or another, there is no way of
coaxing reality to assume an apparently moral aspect,
and when humor itself fails to exorcise evil, one thing
remains for the Englishman to do—that is to come to
blows with the recalcitrant element, in other words to
fight, paying no heed to expostulation. As Lieutenant

Dundas said: "I had a discussion . . . . one day in Oxford with one of those men with a dirty hat and a ready-made tie who come and make speeches on Saturdays in the public squares. He was hurling invective at the aristocracy, the University, and the world at large. Well, after several minutes, I entered the circle and said to him, 'Take off your coat, man, we're going to get to the bottom of the question.'—'Did you convince him, Dundas?'—'Without much difficulty, ... because I really could use my left better than he could.' "[31]

To argue with an Englishman is generally of no avail, since all his behavior is determined not, as in the case of the Frenchman, by various intellectual concepts subject to the influence of reasoning and therefore capable of adjustment, but by a set of fixed principles which are hardly ever to be questioned or altered by power of reasoning. These principles undoubtedly have their roots in the substratum of feelings and sentiments forming the basis of English character. They receive formal and definite expression as a code through the conjoint influence of "public schools" and universities. "Public schools" and universities in England are not altogether centers of learning, as are the corresponding institutions in France. Their purpose is primarily the formation of character. This, according to the English idea, is understood to mean fundamentally the inculcation into young minds of a few precise, standard principles. These principles, which are generally of the most conventional nature, are designed, by their application, to render human relationships as smooth and easy as possible by eliminating all manifestations of

[31] *Les Discours du Docteur O'Grady*, pp. 56–57.

individual tendencies that might prove offensive to others and by relieving the individual of the troublesome and painful uncertainty as to what is the proper conduct to adopt in any situation in which a man may find himself. "We are not going to college in order to study but in order to impregnate ourselves with the prejudices of our class, without which we would be dangerous and unhappy."[32]

In the old established universities, the men who acquire a remarkable degree of erudition and intellectual refinement form a minority. They do not set the tone of the place, as the public understands that tone, and very often they are not the men destined to play a leading part in the national life of England. In this respect nothing fills a learned Frenchman with more amazement than the lack of scholarly interest shown by the average run of students in English universities of the highest standing. "Last night I met a young Englishman who had just spent two years at Cambridge. I tried to speak to him of some remarkable professors I know there. He didn't even know their names. . . . . Then he complained of the new generation which, being spoilt by dancing and the advent of the small car, 'refuses,' he said, 'to work for the college.' In his mouth the word 'work' surprised me. I asked him what he meant. He meant playing Rugby."[33] For such young men, learning or even the cultivation of an ideology is like a difficult and pointless acrobatic feat. They have no use for such pursuits, believing that at school they will already have acquired something more important: a code of behavior which

[32] *Les Silences du Colonel Bramble*, p. 14.
[33] *Conseils à un jeune Français*, pp. 9–10.

they will follow almost blindly for the rest of their lives. *"Instruit dès l'école dans les préjugés qui devront guider sa vie, il considère ... le jeu des idées comme une acrobatie spirituelle."*[34]

The standards which rule the conduct of the Englishman throughout his life, so Maurois would suggest, have no rational or logical basis; they rest almost exclusively upon traditional experience. In the Englishman's view any custom that has endured and has stood the test of time has proved thereby its intrinsic value. Indeed the English believe that the test of time is the only safe guaranty man can have of the soundness of any institution or procedure. "The institutions our ancestors have adopted after six thousand years' experience are worth more than the hasty constructions of silly and pretentious innovators."[35]

The part played by sport in English education and national life is a source of wonder and amazement to practically all foreigners. Maurois, in analyzing the nature of sport in England, discerns with great subtlety several distinct elements. The most obvious is the need for physical exercise, which is indispensable to health in a very damp and rather cold climate. This aspect of the question does not call for any special explanation, as it would be easy to find its counterpart in almost any country with analogous climatic conditions. More curious is the candid, childlike love of play generally betrayed in the Englishman's devotion to sport. This is a perennial source of surprise to the cultured adult of France. Even Maurois, usually so full of sympathy toward English customs, cannot conceal his astonish-

[34] *Les Discours du Docteur O'Grady,* p. 260.
[35] *Ibid.,* pp. 172–73.

ment at the importance attached by apparently sensible men to the act of "pushing a little ball with a stick of a special, elaborate shape" or of "running after animals" or of "passing a ball with the foot or the hand along a line of men in motion."[36] Emphasizing this almost unbridgeable gulf between the French and the English mentalities on this score, Maurois recalls what befell Aristide Briand when, at the instigation of Lloyd George, he decided to take up golf; he, who had been for some time the almost uncontested leader of French foreign policy, at once became the butt of the sarcasm of every French cartoonist: Briand was playing golf! Very rapidly he lost the confidence of the French nation at large; one and all were convinced that his attempt at sport could signify only one thing—the approach of second childhood. In England a political leader who did not play any game would be looked upon with suspicion and distrust. *"Lorsque M. Aristide Briand se mit à jouer au golf avec M. Lloyd George, ce fut la fin d'Aristide Briand. En Angleterre, si le ministre des Affaires Étrangères ne jouait à aucun jeu l'opinion publique s'inquiétérait."*[37]

However, the naïve enjoyment of the game is not, according to Maurois, the most important side of the Englishman's love of sport. The essential point, as far as he is concerned, is that every sport rests upon a set of conventions or arbitrary rules which are accepted not because they are convenient, pleasant, or rational but because they are the rules of the game. Half-humorously, yet with full appreciation of their point of view

[36] *Les Anglais*, p. 55.
[37] A. Maurois, "Le Caractère Anglais," *Conferencia*, April 15, 1937, No. IX, p. 471.

as sportsmen, Maurois attributes the following dialogue to two British officers in the war: " 'To bomb an open city is almost as unforgivable as to try to catch a trout with a worm or to shoot a fox with a gun.'—'You must not exaggerate, Parker,' said the Colonel coolly, 'they [the Germans] have not gone that far yet.' "[38] Indeed, the most momentous steps are often taken by the English much less with the definite idea of furthering their own interests than because of an obscure but powerful instinct to adhere to the rules and the ideals of sport. "If you want to make a Frenchman interested in a boxing match, you must tell him that the nation's honor is at stake; to make an Englishman really interested in a war there is nothing like suggesting to him that it resembles a boxing match."[39]

Even in the daily routine of life, most of the innumerable conventions which so strictly regulate the outward behavior of the Englishman, according to Maurois, are largely traceable to a sporting origin. For instance, the personality of players in a game should never be of any account, nor should the individual's feelings be vented on any occasion. The same rules apply in England to conversation: "Conversation among the British is a game like cricket or boxing: personal allusions are forbidden just as is hitting below the belt, and whoever brings passion into a discussion is immediately disqualified."[40]

Sport conceived of in this way is the occupation par excellence of the English "gentleman." The "gentleman" was a great discovery to many Frenchmen during the war. Though in France people of great intellectual

[38] *Les Silences du Colonel Bramble*, p. 11.
[39] *Ibid.*, p. 10.   [40] *Ibid.*, p. 60.

refinement and high moral standards are by no means
lacking, the original combination of simple yet definite
qualities that make a "gentleman" is not found there
to any great extent, as a regular product of society and
education, although it may exist in some individual
cases as the outcome of personal disposition or of particular circumstances. When the French came into
contact with the British it slowly dawned on the former
that these special features of character, which seemed
to them at first sight somewhat negative, were in fact
the fruit of a long cultural evolution. In spite of his
generally quite obvious intellectual limitations, the
English "gentleman" completely won both the sympathy and the respect of the French people on account
of his staunch, fair, and often kindly attitude toward
life in general, possibly also because of the strict code
of elaborate conventions tending to isolate him from
the warmer but perhaps cruder strain of ordinary human beings. Maurois accurately expresses the feeling
of the French when he says: "A gentleman, a real
gentleman, you see, is very nearly the most engaging
type that has yet been produced by the evolution of the
pitiful group of mammals now creating some stir on
the earth. In the midst of the frightful wickedness of
the species, the English establish an oasis of courtesy
and mutual indifference. Other men may detest one
another; the English merely ignore each other."[41]

English gentlemen—and also many Englishmen
who, for one reason or another, are not quite entitled
to that description—are well aware, often too well
aware, of their own importance. Generally they will
discreetly allow their superiority to be inferred. Occa-

[41] *Ibid.*, p. 46.

sionally, however, some naïve and spontaneous remark of theirs will amusingly betray the very excellent opinion they have of themselves. For example, Maurois quotes[42] the following statement appearing in an English guide-book: "Every Englishman travelling on the Continent must remember that outside Britain all chauffeurs drive on the wrong side of the road."

This self-complacency of the English may be exasperating to foreigners. Maurois, however, wants to see its pleasant side and its favorable consequences. According to him, English pride has this marked virtue: it is the chief source of English tolerance. The British possess such unshakable self-confidence that criticisms directed against them, or misdemeanors 'on the part of other people inspire them with nothing but pity. Their contempt for others makes them almost incapable of real hatred toward those unlike themselves. They feel rather sorry for any unfortunate who has not had the luck to be born an Englishman—or to be a gentleman. Far from resenting divergencies in opinions or manners, they are prepared to make all necessary allowances for the shortcomings of others. Where some nationalities would display anger and be unable to refrain from interfering and trying to put things right according to their own views, the English merely show condescending indifference. Lieutenant Dundas had adopted a disreputable mongrel, called Dick, who got himself into all sorts of scrapes in and about the officers' mess. More than once his master had to apologize to the General for his bad behavior. " 'I am very much afraid, sir,' said he, 'that this fellow, Dick, is not quite a gentle-

---

[42] A. Maurois, "Le Caractère Anglais," *Conferencia*, April 15, 1937, No. IX, p. 464.

man.'—'He is a French dog,' replied General Bramble, indulgently but sorrowfully."[43]

The candid French reader would be greatly mistaken in assuming that all or even most Englishmen actually resemble the characters portrayed in *Bramble* or *O'Grady*. Only a few of them—very few, indeed— bear a likeness to the prototypes depicted by Maurois. These few correspond to a very definite and limited class of men—who are, in fact, of the kind Maurois met most frequently in the course of his duties as interpreter with the staff of the British Army. They were generally recruited from among *public school boys*, many of them being *Oxford* or *Cambridge men*, and they belonged to the type made famous a generation ago by Kipling.

When he came into direct personal contact with the English during the war, Maurois was just passing through a severe moral crisis. His activities in connection with the British Army created a diversion and relieved the strain on his mind, giving him a new zest for life. Thus his English experiences became indissolubly linked with the sentiment of moral recovery and definitely tinged with the pleasant feeling attached to such exhilarating impressions. Moreover, imbued as he was with a deep reverence for convention and tradition—though he chafed under the restraints imposed upon his tendencies and desires by the special forms of convention and tradition which reigned in his French environment—he discovered in himself an unexpected and almost complete affinity with the British. Their sense of the conventional and the traditional was in perfect harmony with his own; yet the particular set

[43] *Les Discours du Docteur O'Grady*, p. 49.

of conventions and traditions that ruled them could
not in any way seem offensive to him personally or in
the least threaten his freedom, since, being peculiar to
the British, they exercised no coercive power over his
French mind.

The combined effect of all these traits was to make
him project into his framework of English life all the
desires which he had failed to realize in France. England became for him a realm of Queen Mab to which
he could escape—metaphorically speaking—and where
he could find compensation for all the disappointments
of real life. To him England truly is, as he himself
suggests[44] by his epigraph at the beginning of *Bramble*:

"This land of such dear souls, this dear, dear land,
This blessed spot, this earth, this realm, this
    England."

His England, however, is not at all an imaginary
and fictitious construction. The description he gives
of English character is built up of solid, objective elements—the results of precise, keen, and shrewd observation and study on the part of a positive and practical
man; but these elements are cemented and unified by
the indefinable yet strong feeling of affection and idealistic sympathy with which they are regarded by Maurois
himself. Hence the half-humorous, half-sentimental
tone that Maurois adopts when speaking about England. His humor covers the blemishes of reality; and
Maurois becomes discreetly sentimental whenever he is
describing some new point of resemblance between English practices and his own desires. This does not impair
the perspicacity, the subtlety, the pointed cleverness of

[44] *Les Silences du Colonel Bramble*, p. 7.

his presentation, but gives it a personal accent all its own.

Several years after the appearance of *Bramble* and *O'Grady* literary fame brought Maurois into contact with an entirely different English type. On his visits to England he was introduced into various sets of modernistic young men and women, some from recognized "society," others from artistic Bohemia. In *Le Côté de Chelsea* Maurois presented a few impressions of this younger generation of literary Britons. Obviously, although keenly interested, he failed to feel toward them the same warm sympathy that he had experienced among the less sophisticated and more natural types of the older England with which he had previously been associated. The very fact that he chose as his mouthpiece in this book the solemn and rather ridiculous diplomat, M. de Norpois, a character from Proust's *A la Recherche du Temps Perdu,* suffices to show that he was regarding them not without serious misgivings. Indeed, the sterling qualities of a Bramble or a Parker are not very apparent among the members of this newer set. So Maurois' feelings are a mixture of curiosity and concern—his concern diminishing, however, with the gradual realization that these young people are but a small minority, powerless against the solid weight of English tradition.

Maurois depicts them as a little clan, refined, oversophisticated, and extremely fastidious. They prize intellectual achievement very highly. Their taste is generally delicate and pure, their erudition sometimes unbelievably rich and varied. However, when they refer to such topics as may give evidence of their knowledge and learning, they assume, lest they should appear pedantic, an air of indifference and nonchalance. Their conversation therefore is often reduced to a series of casual hints and allusions, extremely mystifying and disconcerting to the uninitiated. References on the part of Maurois to their moral standards are conspicuous by their absence . . . . There are no clear-cut profiles in *Le Côté de Chelsea.* On the other hand, a new element, lacking in *Bramble* and *O'Grady,* pervades this book: the atmosphere of London and of the English countryside—a soft, misty, poetical atmosphere, investing all his descriptions with a strange, evocative power and an enduring, captivating charm.

3

INTERPRETATIVE
BIOGRAPHIES

HAVING presented in *Bramble* and *O'Grady* a consistent picture of English character as it had been revealed to him during the war, Maurois felt impelled to go on exploring the complexities and profundities of the English mind and temperament. Very soon he seems to have become aware that his first description of the British, exact and true as it was within its limited scope, did not by any means exhaust the whole content of that infinitely complicated and variegated reality. The plain and solid qualities of character he had so much admired were but a strong and imposing façade masking an extensive labyrinth in intricate problems, puzzling contradictions, and harassing perplexities that lay hidden behind. There was no question of Maurois attempting a general outline or a simplified interpretation of these obscure elements in their powerful and confusing entirety. He had to content himself with drilling a few holes through the veneer of English discipline and composure in order to glance at the tangled mass of aspirations and cravings—the torments of sin, the struggles for individual self-realization, the ferments of revolt against convention, the wild upsurgings of unregulated intelligence, the dull and painful throb of suppressed desires—all those evidences of our common humanity which he found lurking in the stream of English consciousness.

The inferences which he came to draw about the English mind and character Maurois presented in his biographical works. Strikingly, this delineator of English types did not choose as the subjects of his biographies men who could be considered as "typically" English—that is to say, who conformed, if only outwardly, to a certain definite pattern of conventional behavior. Shelley, Disraeli, Byron, and even to a large extent Edward VII were regarded by their contemporaries as exceptional personalities among Englishmen. Through the medium of these special cases Maurois succeeded in bringing to light certain fundamental but obscure and rarely acknowledged features of the English mind. Many Englishmen would challenge the bearing and value of such fragmentary pictures. Conventional Englishmen like to fancy themselves as possessing the traits of a well-bred gentleman like Bramble rather than as wearing the disturbing aspect of a Lord Byron. But in many of them a secret Byronic strain does exist under a smooth surface of Kiplingesque fortitude and balance. When, after the sketches of *Colonel Bramble*, Maurois endeavored to portray Shelley, Disraeli, and Byron, he simply tried, in all honesty, to let us catch a glimpse of the other side of the picture, a side which is as a rule either kept carefully concealed or casually discounted as being in no way representative of what is officially supposed to be the true spirit of England.

In delving thus into hidden realities, Maurois eventually unearthed many unexpected and unsavory facts. Yet in his sincere quest for truth, he displayed the same open mind and loyal sympathy which he had shown in his first studies of English character. Whenever in the course of his investigations he found manifestations of conflicts, errors, and doubts, of a spirit of revolt and even perversity, he tried to understand them and to explain them in terms of the deep and broad experience which he himself had acquired from life. Hence the profound, human appeal of his English biographies. It may be said that Maurois' first pictures of English character, though brilliant and clever, often bear a certain coldness, arising perhaps from Maurois' original assumption of too much perfection and a too well-sustained self-assurance on the part of his types. His biographies, which form the second stage of his experience of the English mind, deal with types warm with passion and suffering, pulsating with struggle, failure, or triumph. Through the portrayal of such types we are brought into intimate contact with very human persons, sometimes courageous and reckless, though often just putting on a brave air—but still more often thoroughly perplexed and blindly groping along their uncertain way. Thus Maurois' biographies, over and above their value as studies of English character, come to have a broader human bearing.

As a matter of fact, Maurois has not confined himself exclusively to biographies of the English; he has written a life of Turgeniev, a life of Marshal Lyautey, the conqueror of Morocco, and even a lengthy sketch of Voltaire. But his biographies of famous Englishmen are by far the best of his biographical works. Maurois' biographies are linked in more than one respect with England and English culture. In English literary tradition biography has long held an honorable place. Maurois, who was well acquainted with English literature, knew the work of the great biographers, such as Trevelyan, John Forster, Lewes, and Strachey. When he himself became a biographer, it was natural that he should follow, whether consciously or unconsciously, in their footsteps; for there was no such tradition in French literature.

Among the French a biography was generally conceived of as a piece of erudite information or as a vehicle for discussion or apologetics. Biography written with the sole object of telling a man's life story, of resurrecting him, as it were, for the sake of studying his personality, was not an established literary *genre*. Very few great French authors ever resorted to biographical writing. But with Maurois' conspicuous success biography became the fashion, and the French literary market has been recently inundated with biographical works. Maurois undoubtedly was among the inaugurators of this new literary trend in France, and if only for that he would deserve special mention in a history of contemporary French literature.

The first quality that our modern, scientifically minded generation requires in a biographer is scrupulous accuracy; and André Maurois has complied with this requirement. Before writing the biography of any of his great men, he has made a careful study of the available documents concerning both the man himself and his social and historical background. Sometimes one may not agree with Maurois' interpretation of the facts, but in regard to the facts themselves Maurois is always on firm ground. Every one of his biographical works rests upon a solid foundation of conscientious study and research; and there is no doubt that in this respect Maurois has come as near to objective scientific truth as is humanly possible.

Maurois himself asks, "*Existe-il, en biographie, une*

vérité scientifique?[1] Is it really possible to know the truth about a man by dint of meticulous and systematic investigation? The bare facts can in many instances be fairly accurately ascertained; but facts in themselves are not all-important in the moral record of a man's life, and it is on the interpretation of the facts that the success of the biography depends. Ten different witnesses may give ten different and widely divergent accounts of the same occurrence. Which, if any, is the correct one? Some documents, such as personal diaries or private letters, would seem to be a comparatively reliable source of information; nevertheless, utilization of such material requires great tact and discrimination on the part of the biographer, since quite unimportant, passing moods or thoughts may often have been recorded and unduly emphasized. The question too of the sincerity of the writer and the problem of suppressed feelings finding an indirect and misleading expression in spite of the writer himself involve the biographer in a maze of complicated difficulties, of critical valuation. In order to extricate himself he has to resort willynilly to the uncertainties of personal intuition for want of a surer method. In such an event, as Maurois points out, "It would be useless and dangerous to try to establish too close a parallelism between the exact and the historical sciences. 'Is it possible to know the truth about a man?' we asked at the beginning. No: one can make an attempt to fix these changing shades . . . . but it is a truth of quite a different character from that pursued by the chemist or the physicist."[2] Should a biographer therefore neglect the

[1] A. Maurois, *Aspects de la Biographie*, Au Sans Pareil, Paris, 1928, p. 91.
[2] *Ibid.*, p. 112.

kind of information that a scientific method can procure? Not at all. The biographer should employ any method that may be applicable in order to arrive at the truth: *"La vérité? Oui, nous devons la poursuivre de toute notre âme."*[3] For that very reason, it is when scientific methods fail that artistic divination should be resorted to.

In Maurois' view one of the most important parts of the biographer's task is to discover by intuition the spirit and the general aim of the life he is studying. He believes that, notwithstanding many apparent contradictions, there is a fundamental harmony in every human existence. It is a harmony that has no relation to strict logic; it may best be compared to the definite yet supple tonalities found in music. Life is "a confused mixture of actions, thoughts and feelings, which are often contradictory to one another, and yet it possesses a unity that is rather like a keynote in music. Your life may be written in C minor or in A major."[4] *"Faire chanter cette note unique et vraie"*[5]—this is the task which the biographer must undertake; and if he is successful, he will have discovered a truth more profound than scientific truth—he will have attained poetic truth.

It very often happens that the man himself during his own life is not consciously aware of that keynote to which his destiny is attuned. As a rule it is only after the last act has been played that the evolution of the human drama becomes apparent and its undulating course can be discerned and traced by the artist. Once the general trend has been ascertained, there is no difficulty in placing every incident and every event in its proper relation to the broad development of action,

---

[3] *Aspects de la Biographie*, p. 112.   [4] *Ibid.*, p. 111.   [5] P. 112.

thought, and feeling leading ultimately to success or failure. The biographer therefore seems perfectly justified in forming his own conceptions of the events in the life story he is narrating and in marshalling them accordingly. In this he must not merely follow the dictates of his own fancy or set out to prove some arbitrary thesis—he must express only what intuition has made him sincerely believe to be the deep and hidden meaning of the man's whole activity.

The biographer's intervention, however, should not be carried out in a manner too obvious or self-assertive. Maurois in his biographical works so carefully erases the lines of construction which he has followed in setting up the whole picture that, though the reader may be conscious of an elaborate internal organization, he does not always realize exactly how it is achieved; he forgets that it is only a picture of life that is being offered him, and comes to accept its rhythm as the pulsation of life itself. Biography is unquestionably a manifestation of true art, and what Maurois says about Strachey could fittingly be applied to himself: *"Le biographe est l'égal du grand musicien et du grand poète."*[6]

If, then, a biography is a work of art, it must stand in close relation to the personality of the artist, the biographer himself. It is not possible for a biographer, however talented, to write the life story of any great man whom he may choose at random and to do so successfully. There must be a definite affinity between the writer and his subject. The biographer, Maurois believes, must himself have gone through moral experiences in many respects similar to those of the man he

6 *Ibid.*, p. 88.

is writing about. It is not necessary—in fact it is hardly possible—that the two should have met with the same adventures; but the problems which confronted the one should have been present in some form and at some particular time in the life history of the other. If this is not the case, the biographer may be able to give an accurate account of events; but the narrative will then inevitably prove to be a mere outline without warmth or feeling, since it will lack the sympathetic vibration of true understanding. The ideal situation for the biographer, according to Maurois, is one in which he finds a reflection or perhaps an earlier manifestation of his own personality in the character he is describing. In that case he is really writing about himself when discussing the other man, and thus his words are endowed with intense sincerity and even with genuine poetry.

The interpretation of documents under these circumstances is an easy matter for the biographer. Signs of conflict and hesitation, outbursts of feeling, mendacious statements, which he may find recorded in memoirs, letters, or other documents, are merely landmarks on a road that he himself has traveled. It is not difficult for him to fill in the gaps between two testimonies or to divine the mental attitude that lies behind some puzzling circumstance. The knowledge gained through his own experience upholds him in the face of apparent contradictions, enabling him to understand intuitively every obscure event and also to give it adequate expression.

In so doing, the biographer himself finds positive relief. It is possible that subconsciously there may remain unsolved questions, thwarted ambitions, unfulfilled dreams of long ago, that are fermenting in his mind and slowly vitiating it. The intensive study and

formal exposition of a similar case serves as an outlet
for all such accumulated emotions and "the work gushes
out from him with an almost spontaneous force."[7]
This applies not to biography alone but also to sincere
endeavor in any branch of art. Yet, before Maurois,
biography was generally regarded as the type of literary work that offered least scope for individual expression of feelings, since it purported to describe only
events connected with another and different personality with which the writer might be sometimes quite
out of sympathy. When Maurois declares that biography should serve the writer as a vehicle for the out-
pouring of his suppressed emotions and desires he nar-
rows its field, since history can provide but a limited
number of cases analogous to that of any given biographer. The biographer, then, may treat successfully
a few people of kindred experience but will fail with
any others. Yet biography gains tremendously from
André Maurois' conception, for it gains life itself; and
the very essence of biography is the re-creation of real
life. Biography is not a cold or dead thing; it is a living
integration of the emotions of two men, separated
physically in space and in time but united by common
joys and sufferings. Sentiments of affection, repulsion,
or pity may be uttered legitimately by the biographer,
since this type of creative work has now become a means
of personal expression.

In most of Maurois' biographical works it is easy to
discern the personal link of common moral experience
between the author and his hero, also to isolate the leading idea around which Maurois has organized facts he
had to present; and it is even generally possible to see

[7] *Aspects de la Biographie,* p. 119.

how far Maurois has carried out the fundamental work
of research and investigation in order to get as near as
can be to the ever elusive and yet ever alluring "scientific" truth.

Maurois himself has told what prompted him to
write a biography of Shelley—apparently for him a
rather unexpected choice: "When for the first time I
read a short life of Shelley, I experienced a keen emotion. The reason for this was as follows: I had just
left the 'Lycée,' filled with political and philosophical
ideas which represented fairly closely—save for the
difference in our respective eras—the ideas entertained
by Shelley and his friend Hogg at the time of their
arrival in London. Then, suddenly impelled to action
by circumstances, I had found my ideas in conflict with
my experience. I had wanted to apply to my emotional
life the rational systems which I had conceived ab-
stractly in studying the great philosophers; I had encountered on all sides living and sentient matter which
did not yield to my logic. I had caused suffering and I
myself had suffered. I felt irritated with the youth
that I had formerly been and also indulgent toward
him. . . . . I wanted at once to expose, to condemn and
to explain him. . . . . Now Shelley had experienced
mental frustration and failure which seemed to me to
be somewhat similar to my own. . . . . Yes, indeed, it
appeared to me that in telling the story of his life I
might to some extent unburden myself. . . . . Be it
good or bad, the book was written with pleasure, with
passion."[8]

The facts to which Maurois here refers—his youthful enthusiasm for the altruistic theories instilled into

[8] *Aspects de la Biographie*, pp. 123–25.

him by Chartier and his subsequent difficulties when he tried to apply them both at the cloth factory and during his first matrimonial venture—these facts do not present to an outside observer any very striking similarity to Shelley's early experiences; but that Maurois should have felt the affinity was sufficient to justify and to explain the throb of personal emotion which they aroused in him.

The main theme of the book is clearly the minor tragedy that occurs in the moral evolution of so many young men. Almost every serious-minded youth will sooner or later conceive some marvelous plan to reform the world and make it a happier place to live in. The system, so it would appear, is always very ingeniously contrived to solve a great many of the complicated problems with which unfortunate humanity has been contending for generations or for centuries. The sheltered and secluded intellectual atmosphere of college is a highly favorable medium for the breeding and development of such idealistic theories. However, in due time, the student comes into contact with reality, which obstinately refuses to fit in with theories or conform to systems. When the young idealist tentatively applies his doctrines to conditions over which he may chance to have some control, those concerned are at first hurt and displeased, and thereafter they react violently against the proposed reforms; so it usually happens that before long the beautiful scheme breaks down completely, sometimes carrying the would-be reformer to destruction with it. In most cases, however, when the dreamer realizes the impossibility of putting his theories into practice, he comes to the conclusion that academic teaching is at fault, and forthwith applies his energies to some work of a more practical nature. What

Maurois sets out to show is that the youthful spirit of reform, disinterested and idealistic as it may be, invariably comes to grief when it encounters hard, cruel reality. After this painful impact and the resulting catastrophe, the soul like a troubled sea is for long strewn with the debris of lost dreams, and far beneath the surface lies the wreck of youthful hopes.

By the time Maurois came to write the story of Shelley's moral tragedy, he was somewhat out of sympathy with unpractical, young idealists like the poet. He scoffed at Shelley's efforts—hence the somewhat ironical tone that permeates the biography. This vein of irony adds humor to the story, although it is apt to convey the impression that the author is taking sides against his young hero. The recollections of his own experiences were still fresh in his mind; and he may have drawn on them for the imaginary dialogues with which he enlivened the narrative and which are in conformity with psychological truth although they have no historical foundation. Yet he never distorted history in any other way. The facts presented are perfectly exact, and are based obviously on reliable information which he had collected carefully and to which he adhered accurately. Maurois brought no fresh document to light; the facts were already well known. In the choice of these established facts, Maurois, perhaps because he is French, gave exceptional prominence to those connected with women and love, and neglected more or less those related to poetry; but, presented with hardly any reference to his poetry, the poet frequently appears merely as a slightly extravagant eccentric.

Indeed no work of Maurois conveys a more vivid impression of phantasmagoria. The facts of Shelley's

life are all given with precision; their motivation, however, is either so fantastic or so sublime that they seem
to develop much more on the plane of a daydream than
on the plane of earthly reality. Such is the unreal spirituality permeating the "crystalline" figure of the poet,
and suffusing all his actions, that the reader, when clos-
ing the volume, cannot help but wonder whether he
has been made acquainted with a creature of flesh and
blood or if he has just been expected to admire the disconcerting appearances of some immaterial being. The
title of "Ariel" which Maurois gave to his book is suf-
ficent evidence that he intended quite consciously to
conjure up about his hero an atmosphere of ethereal
and elusive quality. Whether or not this half-ironical
narrative fully accounts for the actual deportment of
Shelley the man may certainly be questioned. However, when following the unusual behavior of the young
poet, in his married life and among his friends, the
reader cannot bring himself to feel critically inclined.
He is carried along by the irresistible flow of clever
conversations, graceful episodes, surprising turns of
events—exactly as he would be by the imaginary plot
of an entertaining novel. The book indeed reads like a
novel, and that is why its defects almost as much as its
merits contributed to make of this biography an in-
stantaneous success.

In the case of *La Vie de Disraëli* the question of the
personal bond between the writer and his subject is
rather more complex. Emile-Salomon-Wilhelm Herzog
had had occasionally to contend with the same anti-
Jewish prejudice that had impeded young Disraeli
when he tried to win his way into society. "I had great
sympathy for Disraeli as he became aware of the oppo-
sition of a hostile world—for the man so grossly at-

tacked by such mediocre adversaries."[9] This created
a link between the two personalities. Then again,
Maurois' politics, in which conservatism—the outcome
of a provincial environment and a family tradition—is
judiciously mingled with progressiveness traceable to
the influence of Chartier, had actually much in common with the Tory democracy of the English statesman. "It seemed to me that through him I could express a political doctrine which was exactly what I was
seeking—I mean a democratic conservatism—the blending of a great respect for tradition, for all that has
been acquired by humanity in the past, with a solicitude
for the happiness of all classes and a desire for orderly
reform. Since I was myself unable for manifold reasons to lead a life of political activity, I derived a
passionate pleasure from participating in that struggle
behind the mask of a political figure that so appealed
to me."[10]

Lastly, in Maurois there has always been, on the one
hand, a romantic idealist, craving a full, free existence;
on the other hand, a man of experience, well aware of
the restraints of practical life. The same contradictory
elements were present in the character of Disraeli.
"The more I read, the more I felt that I might find in
Disraeli a hero in whom I could be passionately interested. I was dealing with a type of character that was
new to me, the romantic who is at the same time a man
of action."[11] Here Maurois utilized all the facts to
show how important this romantic tendency was in
Disraeli's life, just as it was in his own. In the hearts
of some men, as Maurois says, there is an inexhaustible
store of romantic potentialities. Such men have a taste

---

[9] *Aspects de la Biographie*, p. 126.
[10] *Ibid.*, p. 126.   [11] *Ibid.*, p. 125.

for high adventure; they are willing to take risks in a noble cause—even if it be nought but a beautiful dream, impossible of fulfillment. These selfless dreamers often become entangled in the petty interests and prejudices of average humankind. Then their visions may be deemed madness and their activity end in dismal failure. Yet nothing great is ever achieved on earth that has not first been conceived by some romantic visionary. An inspired leader may persuade a whole nation to forget its practical interests and follow him. Thus did Disraeli present to his generation the vision of an Empire. A vision is never of long duration; reality soon claims the undivided attention of the man in the street, and in the long run common sense returns. But even if nothing practical comes of it, the dream has not been in vain if it has been a source of inspiration and exaltation to many.

The problem dealt with in *La Vie de Disraëli* is in a manner similar to that considered in *Ariel*, involving the conflict between idealism and reality. But, whereas Maurois saw in Shelley the prototype of the theorizing young man who tries unsuccessfully to force reforms on living people, he portrays Disraeli as the impenitent romantic who seeks to breathe the spirit of life into inert masses and outworn institutions. That Maurois felt in sympathy with his hero is obvious. The tone of irony or latent hostility that characterizes the Shelley biography is not introduced into *La Vie de Disraëli*, except perhaps in passages dealing with Gladstone. More than once it would seem as if Maurois, in bringing to light the dazzling career of a man of his own race, were enjoying vicariously the very achievements by which he himself had set the greatest store but which he had been unable in his own case to realize.

Thus he evidently revels in Disraeli's amazing personal triumphs in society; he delights in his brilliant oratory; he seems even to share in his matrimonial happiness, resting upon a perfectly harmonious sentimental association; but, above all, he admires Disraeli's successful combining of practical activity with unbridled imagination—thus solving a problem which had confronted Maurois himself for many years but for which his own experience had provided no solution.

Maurois, however, is always exceedingly tactful in the expression of his sentiments. He shows equally good taste and discretion in his representation of Disraeli's private life. In this respect the book is a masterpiece, wherein the personal elements and public achievements are cleverly blended into a consistent and harmonious whole. The book, moreover, is founded on incontestable documentary evidence and upon an intimate knowledge of all the characters, of their historical setting, and of the society in which they lived and moved. Imaginary dialogues such as enlivened *Ariel* have no place in *La Vie de Disraëli*. The subtle charm inherent in the portrayal of a kindred personality intuitively understood, the wide general appeal of a romantic character striving to create a new and better world, the sure basis of a sound erudition, all combine to make this biography in all probability André Maurois' masterpiece.

In *Byron* the personal link is not at first sight so easily discernible. Yet Byron's life seems to have held some of the very problems which Maurois himself had to face during the period of his first marriage, when he found himself morally tied and almost paralyzed by the narrow traditions and strict conventions which prevailed among the provincial *bourgeoisie* of his native place. He must often have felt tempted to break all the accepted rules and gain personal freedom. Still more impatient than he himself was his gifted and brilliant wife, who chafed at the petty regulations and the hypocritical conventions of that small circle, to which she in no wise belonged. She wanted openly to flout the gossip-mongers and to be really herself. That is precisely what Byron did—in very different circumstances, of course, but in a spirit that Maurois could easily imagine and that he longed to re-create.

The general idea which the book seeks to convey is that disaster inevitably awaits all those who, like Byron, cast off the shackles of convention and blindly follow their natural impulses. The disaster is not, Maurois thinks, the outcome of outside pressure brought to bear by society upon one who violates the social code, though the effects of that pressure are by no means negligible.

The real cause of the downfall is in the internal conflict between the unleashed, uncontrolled instincts which are given free rein and the obscure aspirations toward order and morality which exist deep down in all men, even in those who suspect it least. If these moral aspirations are entirely thwarted, the fundamental balance of the mind is upset. The victim is afflicted with seemingly causeless melancholy; he suffers mental torture, though he may be outwardly prosperous; and at the end he generally meets with catastrophe.

Maurois worked for ten years on Byron's biography. As the subject was in some points of a very delicate and controversial nature, he took care to display an imposing critical and historical framework. His preliminary study and investigation were more thorough for this than for any of his other books. The story develops smoothly, objectively, impartially, without condemnation or justification; yet it is full of understanding. Maurois invokes modern theory in order to explain the inferiority complex which seems to have tinged all Byron's emotional life. Yet this reference to psychology is a discreet one, and the book never tends to become a mere study of a clinical case. The background is tactfully evoked without being given undue prominence. Byron's poetical genius receives proper attention, and selections of his verse are presented to the French reader in cleverly translated, rhythmical prose. In short, the book is technically very nearly perfect. Nevertheless it is inferior to *La Vie de Disraëli*. It lacks the transforming touch of perfect sympathy. Toward Byron, Maurois seems to cherish a feeling of profound pity, but nothing more.

However, Maurois reveals a Byron much less depraved than tradition has painted him. He sees him as a high-spirited youth, possessed it is true of a dangerous heredity, but by no means lacking in elevated sentiment and instinct. In fact, according to Maurois, Byron seems from the beginning to have been thirsting after the perfection of feminine purity, which he never ceased secretly to revere and worship to the end of his days. But a somber Calvinistic view of religion was early implanted in him, bound up with the haunting idea of unavoidable sin and of predestined, everlasting damnation. Now the humiliation of his crippled leg made him feel at an early age that he was especially marked out from other men by a fateful stigma of inferiority and suffering. It was, however, when with all the desperate violence of a passionate nature he fell in love with Mary Chaworth—and was repulsed by her—that his character and his life took a new turn. In self-defense and revenge against a hostile world with its cruel prejudices and conventions, the oversensitive lad assumed the role of a skeptic and a cynic. His outstanding characteristic was thus "a generous, almost morbid sensitiveness, which, in early youth, must have formed the background for a beautiful character. The chill of wickedness he had felt so precociously had prevented the good seeds from germinating but had not succeeded in killing them. When Byron said he was a fallen angel, he was right. There were in him all the elements of an angel; but he had found man so hard and so false that the horror of hypocrisy had become his dominant instinct."[12]

Then he tried to forget, through sheer intensity of present sensation, his too lofty, impossible dream. Moreover, having suffered at the time of his first overwhelming experience of love the appalling torments of humiliation, frustration, and jealousy combined, he was apt now to find normal, ordinary life hopelessly flat and banal. Just as a traveler who has been initiated into the use of burning, exotic spices afterward finds plain, wholesome food tasteless and insipid, so Byron was condemned to eternal boredom, from which he could not escape except through further excitement and further passion, the very violence and intensity of which completely vitiated and destroyed all moral self-control. And why not? Had he not for many years had an intimate, irresistible conviction of his own doom?

Hence his stormy adventure with Caroline Lamb and his notorious liaison with his half-sister Augusta; hence his misunderstanding with his wife—a thoroughly respectable person to be sure, but none the less thoroughly commonplace and dull, and inevitably falling

---

[12] A. Maurois, *Byron*, Grasset, Paris, 1930, II, 239.

short of the impossibly high ideal of woman which
Byron had once formed; hence also the low kind of
revelry in which he finally indulged in Venice. Nevertheless, even in the midst of this dissipation, higher aspirations were not dead in Byron; when a generous
enthusiasm for Hellenic liberty provided him with a
motive at once disinterested and elevated, his inner
self at last found expression and complete fulfillment
in heroic sacrifice.

The lack of personal affinity between Maurois and
the other men whose life stories he undertook to write
may perhaps account for the indifferent quality of the
remaining biographies. Some of them are in the form of
simple sketches; others have developed into full-length
books, though failing to offer the same human interest
as Maurois' first biographical productions.

Of the sketches, that on Dickens is perhaps the cleverest and the most penetrating. Maurois indicates the
vivid contrast between the prosperity, pride, and ego-
tism of high society in England during the nineteenth
century and the abject poverty of the poorer classes.
Dickens, who in his early days had known what real
distress meant, during all his later life used the weapons
of his literary genius and sympathetic humor to combat
the haunting ghost of this monstrous evil. Yet he never
succeeded altogether in ridding himself of the obses-
sion of this misery. He spent practically all his time trying to escape the memories of his unhappy childhood
and to dull his regret for the sentimental mistakes of his
youth. All those talkative, grinning, and grimacing
characters in his books are, so Maurois fancies, personifi-
cations of his efforts to avoid the tête-à-tête with his
own soul.

The biography of Lyautey was written on the occasion of the Colonial Exhibition in Paris in 1931. In the course of a trip to North Africa in 1925 Maurois had had an opportunity of seeing for himself the astounding achievements of this leader, on whose shoulders had rested the whole burden of the conquest and colonization of Morocco. But though there was in Maurois something of the man of action, and though Lyautey displayed, especially in the planning of the towns that he founded, the instincts and talents of an artist, nevertheless the general and his biographer had little in common. As a result the biography presents a collection of facts, faithfully and vividly recorded, it is true, and yet giving the reader no deep insight into the tremendous personality of the great conqueror.

Turgeniev was a Westernized Russian, of cosmopolitan culture, but still very much a Slav at heart. Maurois found in him some of the Slavic characteristics with which he doubtless had become personally familiar during the period of his married life with Janine de Szymkievicz. These features, then, may be considered to some extent, though indirectly, as part of his own experience. Perhaps this experience was too indirect; or perhaps Turgeniev's habit of "laisser-aller" was a characteristic that did not appeal to Maurois—at all events the picture of Turgeniev seems cold and "external." Yet the Russian environment is suggestively depicted, Turgeniev's intellectual perplexities and inconsistencies are cleverly analyzed, and the evolution of his passion for a married woman, Pauline Viardot, as it gradually turns into friendship, is aptly presented. Nevertheless sympathy is lacking and the book has no fire.

Perhaps it was not altogether a coincidence that, when Maurois was approaching the age at which a man likes to settle down, he chose to write the biography of Edward VII. During the lifetime of Queen Victoria her son had been, to say the least, somewhat independent and impatient of Victorianism; but after his accession he gradually acquired his sense of traditional sovereignty and came to exert a subtle diplomatic influence in Europe, in which pursuit he found the meaning and purpose of his life. All this is well explained in Maurois' book; but for understandable reasons the intimate note is very seldom struck, and the book too often becomes a mere outline of European politics before the World War.

Thus the characteristic features and consequences of Maurois' conception of the biographer's art are clearly apparent. Since biography is conceived by him essentially as a means of expression for the biographer himself, the lives of very few historically or otherwise famous persons can be presented successfully. Indeed the number will be limited to those who have had experiences in some respects similar to the biographer's. In cases where that similarity is completely or almost completely lacking, the biography is little more than a record of facts, which may be objectively sound but in which there is seldom much warmth or personal appeal. When Maurois has been able to find a deeper and more direct affinity between himself and his subject, he has indeed achieved wonders of intuition and creative art.

4

NOVELS BY MAUROIS

FICTION offered Maurois much wider scope than did biography, although it gave him a less sure foundation to build upon. In his biographical writings he was restricted yet at the same time supported, as it were, by the indestructible facts of the life history of an actual person. In his novels it was possible for him to express his own feelings and ideas more directly and to shape the events befalling his fictitious characters according to his personal conception of reality.

Yet it has often been said that Maurois lacked the full power of original creative imagination; and this is to some extent true. Frequently it is possible to trace the essentials of his plots and characters to certain well-known facts and definite sources. Ever since the controversy raised by Auriant in 1928, French literary critics have been wont to look for such sources in every new book of Maurois' that appears. In the case of his biographies, he himself has acknowledged his indebtedness to certain scholarly works which indeed no serious biographer could well afford to ignore. *Le Côté de Chelsea* is a *pastiche* of Proust. Several more or less debatable rapprochements have been made between Alain Gerbault's *Seul à travers l'Atlantique* and Maurois' *Voyage au Pays des Articoles*, between Maurice Baring's *Daphne Adeane* and *Climats*, between *Cat's Cradle* and *Le Cercle de Famille*. Undoubtedly Mau-

rois has in no case consciously adapted to his own use
fragments of some other author's work—as he has been
unjustly accused of doing. However, in view of similarities here and there, it seems possible that certain half-
conscious reminiscences may have found their way into
his most original compositions. In fact, the true originality of André Maurois lies much less in the invention
of completely new, unused material than in the thoroughly personal organization and interpretation of the
elements ready to his hand. The mode of presentation
of these elements and the art of investing them with a
moral or psychological meaning are of course entirely
Maurois' own. The factual elements themselves may
come from a variety of different sources. The starting
point may be the narrative, read in some book, of an
unusual adventure. Thus the first part of the *Voyage
au Pays des Articoles* seems to have been partly inspired
by Gerbault's book. Or, again, a living person, more or
less closely acquainted with the novelist, may have taken
him as a confidant and so have provided him with a
foundation of facts on which he could build freely.

In most cases, however, the actual events of the author's own life can be discerned underlying the general
development of his novels. This gives certain of his
works, especially his earlier books, a deep and moving
appeal. Yet these novels are not by any means to be
considered as fragments of a confession by Maurois
himself. Any private and personal elements they may
contain have been so much elaborated that the reader,
though he may occasionally be aware that the author is
drawing on his past experience, very soon realizes the
futility of looking for any complete and detailed parallelism between Maurois' fiction and the actualities of
his life.

However, Maurois' novels stand in such close relation to his personality that one may find in them the reflection of his chief trends of thought and individual tendencies. Maurois has always kept in touch, on the one hand, with the practical aspects of existence through the multiple links of family tradition and of financial interests, and probably also through an inborn taste for action. On the other hand, his intellectual faculties have delighted to soar unfettered into an imaginative realm of artistic and philosophical fancy. So his novels fall very definitely into two distinct groups.

Certain of them, such as *Ni Ange, ni Bête, Bernard Quesnay, Climats, Le Cercle de Famille,* and *L'Instinct du Bonheur,* offer a quite realistic picture of the familiar French provincial or Parisian environment. They are filled with exact psychological observations and generally deal with the modern world which we all know. Others, such as *Voyage au Pays des Articoles, La Peseur d'Ames,* and *La Machine à Lire les Pensées,* are much more abstract and theoretical; they have an imaginary or decidedly foreign setting and their main theme hinges upon some unlikely and unreal hypothesis. These two different types of literary production do not correspond to two successive stages of Maurois' intellectual progress. The tendencies they represent simultaneously co-exist in his mind; alternately, though irregularly, these tendencies find expression in works of either one type or the other. For the convenience of study, each kind will be examined here separately and distinctly.

Ni Ange, ni Bête belongs to the same period as the biography of Shelley, and it illustrates in like manner the disjunction between real life and abstract theory. The chief character of the book, Philippe Viniès, is a composite of what Maurois himself was before the war, of Shelley at the time of his elopement with Harriet Westbrook, and of a certain young French engineer who was living in Abbeville about 1848. Maurois had come upon documents relating to this man in the archives of this little town and in them found the authentic episodes upon which the story is based. Young Philippe arrives from Paris to take up the office of city engineer. "He is not stupid, but ready-made formulas stand as a screen between his mind and reality; he constructs for himself a universe of petty and rigid systems and would fain have Nature submit to the laws laid down by M. Viniès. He has a theory on Poland, a theory on love, a theory on marriage, ... further a theory on the community of goods, and for each of these he professes himself ready to take up arms."[1] He marries a blonde, a somewhat insipid young person, Geneviève by name. But he very nearly wrecks the marriage by introducing into his home a brother idealist and fellow vegetarian who is also keenly appreciative of Geneviève's charms. He cannot attune himself to the petty interests and prejudices of the little provincial town and would defiantly sweep them out of existence with his grandiose schemes of reform. Finally, after involving himself deeply in the revolutionary movement of 1848, he is only too glad to take refuge in England. The book is certainly not a masterpiece; the characters are little more than intelligent puppets made to express differing points of view. Maurois was still in his literary novitiate.

In *Bernard Quesnay* we find ourselves in an entirely different world, a world of struggle and conflict, inhabited by people of real flesh and blood. At Elbeuf, as a young man, Maurois had been torn between the

---

[1] A Maurois, *Ni Ange, ni Bête*, Grasset, Paris, 1919, p. 18.

claims of a drab industrial career and the longing for a cultured and colorful existence; he had passed through all the sentimental complications involved in the problem, and knew how detrimental it is to a woman's happiness to be tied to a man whose whole attention and energy are engrossed in business. These two questions and the side issues to which they give rise constitute the framework of the book.

In the town of Pont-de-l'Eure (which stands obviously for Elbeuf) the Quesnay family have for generations been the proprietors of a cloth factory. The old grandfather devotes himself exclusively, almost fanatically, to the running of the factory. "Supposing his grandson had asked him: 'What is the use of spending one's brief existence in manufacturing cloth?' He would no doubt have answered: 'What's the use of existing at all if one doesn't manufacture cloth?' Any conversation that did not have reference to the technique of his calling was to him only empty sound."[2] His two grandsons, Antoine and Bernard, are less enthusiastic; nevertheless they do their work conscientiously. It is a dull, monotonous round of duties that they are called upon to face. They have to listen to the ever-recurring complaints of discontented workmen, to humor finical customers, to study an overstocked market, to keep pace with reckless competitors. Occasionally there are strikes to break the monotony, strikes originating over some trivial dispute—then the deadening atmosphere of dull routine soon settles again over the bleak and dingy buildings with their ceaseless hum of engines and looms.

[2] A. Maurois, *Bernard Quesnay*, Nouvelle Revue Française, Paris, 1926, p. 15.

Bernard strikes up a friendship with a charming
Parisienne, Simone. When in Paris he always contrives
a hurried rendezvous with her between pressing business engagements in the city. The two are really in love
with each other; but Bernard is very busy, and his love-
making is limited to those rare occasions when he is able
to detach his mind from thoughts of profits, salaries,
outlays, and other business matters. Simone soon tires
of being of merely secondary interest. Antoine is in
much the same case with regard to his wife, Françoise.
Life with Antoine has nothing to offer—nothing but the
boredom of the humdrum existence led by the inhab-
itants of Pont-de-l'Eure. Françoise tries to rouse him
to take a wider, more colorful view of things. He quite
understands what she is aiming at, but like his brother he
also has no time to spare—he is far too busy. Finally
Simone definitely throws Bernard over, while Antoine
is in danger of being deserted by Françoise. Bernard is
now concentrating on business to the exclusion of all
else; but Antoine is beginning to wonder if he is not
losing more than he is gaining by making the factory
the be-all and end-all of his existence. Realizing at last
that he must choose, he liquidates his share in the factory and retires to the French Riviera. He will have
very little money, it is true; but he will have leisure
for mind and body, and will keep the affection of his
now happy and contented wife. Bernard, who is 'already becoming very much like his grandfather, sternly
disapproves of his brother's move. He feels perhaps
that the best and most fruitful part of his own personality has withered and died within him; but the
factory now constitutes his whole life, and on his grandfather's death he naturally steps into his grandfather's
place.

Bernard and Antoine obviously represent two different sides of Maurois' own character, and also two possible solutions of the great problem that faced him at a certain period of his career. The manifold complexity of a man's soul has been reduced here to two simple, coherent, and consistent attitudes. Their divergent evolution is perhaps a shade too logical, too precise, too symmetrical. The principal merit of the book lies in the striking evocation of the moral and technical aspects of the world of business. The picture is at once so accurate and so intense that it conveys a striking impression of reality and truth. As a matter of fact Maurois had previously written a short study entitled *La Hausse et la Baisse*, which dealt exclusively with the peculiar conditions and the problems pertaining to the man of business. It was published in 1922 in *Les Œuvres Libres*. It ranks as one of his shorter masterpieces. Several years later, after he had left the cloth factory and could see the whole of this part of his life in retrospect, he took up the early sketch, enlarged it, and introduced a few women into the story, with the sentimental complications arising from their presence and their aspirations. Thus in 1926 was produced *Bernard Quesnay*.

But the sentimental complications which Maurois himself experienced found their best expression in *Climats*. Philippe Marcenat, the hero, comes of a highly respected and conventional family. The Marcenats have been established for several generations in the beautiful yet rather severe province of the Limousin, where they are the owners of a prosperous paper mill. They also have a foothold in Paris, because Paris is the center of all commercial transactions in this line of business. Philippe is a partner in the family firm and possesses all the qualities of the perfect businessman. He has a precise, positive, and scientific turn of mind. He is reticent and inclined to be always on the defensive, but is faithful and honorable and proud of the family traditions. Although serious, austere, and sometimes almost puritanic in his ways, he has deep down in him a tenderer and more sensitive strain. He is given to dreaming, is eager for beauty, and is perhaps less stable at bottom than he appears to be. But this part of his personality he keeps carefully suppressed. He marries a brilliant and beautiful girl, Odile Malet, whom he has met during a trip to Italy. She is not a woman of very superior type, but she has spontaneity, force, love of freedom, and a zest for life—all of which qualities are conspicuously lacking in the stern tribe of the Marcenats. That is probably why she has such a tremendous appeal for Philippe. It is also the reason why misunderstandings crop up thick and fast between the two young people almost at the very beginning of their married life. Trifles acquire exaggerated importance because they are the symbols of different moral atmospheres. In reaction against Odile's levity, Philippe is driven to accentuate his devotion to high principles, and becomes more and more unbending and conventional. Odile forms a liaison with a young officer in the navy whom she believes to be as sincerely romantic as herself and who is in fact nothing but an inveterate "lady-killer." Eventually she runs away with him; but, discovering her mistake too late, she shoots herself in despair.

The war comes, years roll by, and Philippe gradually recovers from the shock of Odile's tragic end—so far even as to marry again. But this time he chooses a wife of a different type. Isabelle is a "nice" girl, well brought up, modest, and unassuming. She is both sentimental and practical, and is endowed with all the qualities that ought to make a convention-ridden, family-loving man like Philippe completely happy. Yet he is not happy. He longs for that romantic flavor which Odile could infuse into his life. A new Philippe Marcenat seems to appear in him. He who formerly used to bristle at the disturbing but alluring ways of his first wife now, to the dismay of the second, takes a woman of doubtful repute as his mistress and behaves exactly as if Odile posthumously had converted him to her conception of existence. Then, just as a timely revolver shot has put an end to Odile after her elopement with the naval officer, a sudden attack of pneumonia kills Philippe after he himself has reaped the bitter fruit of his misadventure.

In spite of the stylization of the plot and the somewhat obvious symmetry of the two episodes, there is a strain of deep emotion and sincerity running through the whole book. Its relation to Maurois' own personal experience is self-evident.

The general idea that Maurois here wishes to convey is that every personality carries with it a distinctive moral atmosphere. When we love a person, it means simply that we need the atmosphere surrounding that person. This atmosphere may vary and change; yet throughout it possesses a definite unity, something like the "climate" of a given country—hence the title of the book, *Climats*. And just as the physical climate of a country may mold the personalities of those who live in it, in the same way the moral atmosphere of a person with whom for a long time we are very intimately associated may influence us deeply, even unbeknown to ourselves, to the extent of completely transforming our life. Unfortunately the process of transformation

is usually slow and the changes become evident only
when their causes and the need for them are long past
and over: *"Nos destinées et nos volontés jouent presque
toujours à contretemps."*[3]

Maurois' remaining novels are far from offering the
same gripping human interest as those already mentioned, perhaps because the personal element in them is
much more restricted. In many of them one has the
impression of being face to face with a large and complicated theoretical structure. But the architect is always
clever and the work never fails to be of interest.

Le Cercle de Famille describes the unhappy matrimonial affairs of Louis Herpain, a wool merchant in
Pont-de-l'Eure. Herpain was formerly a brilliant pupil
at the Lycée of Rouen, where he was strongly influenced
by a teacher with decided radical views; but he has
allowed himself to be smothered by the dull conven-
tionality of the small provincial town. In a fit of
romanticism he has married Germaine d'Hocquinville,
the good-looking and gifted daughter of an aristocratic but impecunious family. Soon the whole town is
talking about Germaine's "secret" meetings with a
young Dr. Guérin. One evening Denise, Germaine's
little daughter, by accident sees the doctor kiss her
mother while the two are at the piano, and she never
recovers from the shock.

Denise at once begins to hate her mother and, later,
when she grows up leaves her home at the first opportunity. She goes to Paris to study, and there becomes
engaged to a young man from Pont-de-l'Eure whom
she has known as a boy at school. She tries in vain to
make him share her enthusiasm for an interesting and

[3] A. Maurois, *Climats*, Grasset, Paris, 1928, p. 286.

colorful existence, even though a precarious one financially. When he sensibly accepts a position as a notary
at home in Pont-de-l'Eure, she immediately breaks off
the engagement. Denise continues to go her own way.
Eventually she marries—though not for love—the
weak-willed but enormously wealthy Edmond Holmann, son of a banker. She induces him to invest his
money in some big but fantastic financial schemes, and
so brings about the collapse of the firm. Then she seeks
excitement in clandestine love affairs and seems well
on the way to ultimate ruin and disgrace. However,
suddenly, at a crucial moment, she perceives in her
little daughter, Marie-Laure, the same look of horror
and anguish that must have appeared on her own face
when, as a child years before, she discovered Dr. Guérin
and her own mother together. Thus a family's history
may repeat itself in successive generations. Life runs in
circles: *Le Cercle de Famille.*

The humiliation Denise had felt when she realized
the unworthiness of her own mother had warped her
outlook. Aware, even as a child, of the failure of her
father as a man, she had all her life, by way of compensation, played unconsciously the part of a man herself:
she had studied like a man, had behaved like a man, and
so had quite missed her destiny as a woman. As a man
too she had felt that her mother deserved retribution
for her misconduct. But now, through the irresistible
turn of the wheel of events—another "circle" of the
family history—she was inflicting on her own daughter
the very same wound that had caused her to suffer so
much herself. The full realization of all this checks
her on the brink of a desperate adventure and at the
same time enables her to master her "complex" and so
return to a more normal view of life.

Autobiographical data are used sparingly in this book. Certain personal recollections are easily recognizable at the beginning, but soon the hectic existence led by Denise carries the reader to an altogether different sphere. Toward the end another character appears: one Bertrand Schmitt, a novelist, who is married to Isabelle, the widow of Philippe Marcenat. The Philippe Marcenat of *Climats* had obviously in many respects been an incarnation of André Maurois himself in early life, and Bertrand Schmitt very much resembles Maurois at a later stage of his development. Denise, who had known Schmitt in Pont-de-l'Eure, makes him her confidant. Her confession to him gives the key to her otherwise rather puzzling and disconcerting behavior, likewise a definite clue as to the external origin of the whole story.

The psychological analysis constitutes the most important element in the book. It is conducted with great dexterity and with so much attention to detail that the reader is made to feel as if he were actually threading the maze of sentiments confusing a tormented and unbalanced soul. Yet the very ingenuity of the plot, beginning with a mental shock and then toward the end bringing in a repetition of the same situation, leaves the impression of an almost too artificial cleverness.

Shortly after finishing *Climats* Maurois wrote in his diary: "I am rather sorry that I killed Philippe and that I did not attempt a third part, presenting a picture of happiness. It would have been difficult, no doubt. . . . . I shall try to do this later with other characters."[4] That seems to have been the origin of *L'Instinct du Bonheur*.

Here a wealthy, middle-aged couple, Gaston Romilly and his wife, Colette, who have been settled for

---

[4] A. Maurois, *Mes Songes que voici*, Grasset, Paris, 1933, p. 133.

some time in the province of Périgord, are very much
upset when their daughter, Valentine, falls in love
with a young man of the neighborhood. If a marriage
takes place they will be obliged, in accordance with
French law, to produce their daughter's birth certificate,
and so the girl will learn that she is a natural child,
born before their legal union. They envisage the moral
tragedy that such a revelation will bring about—disgrace in the eyes of their friends and perhaps a public
scandal. Finally, however, through the intervention of
a Mme de la Guichardie, an inveterate matchmaker,
they discover that Valentine has known the truth all
along and is not at all concerned about it; she kept
silent because some secret instinct warned her that it
would be better not to mention the subject. All seems
to be well until, quite unexpectedly, Valentine is left
a large fortune by an elderly man, Martin Bussière, apparently a complete stranger. Colette Romilly is confused with embarrassment. She has always let Gaston
believe that he is the father of Valentine, whereas the
girl's real father is the now troublesome Martin Bussière. This inopportune and incriminating bequest is
undoubtedly going to create suspicion, and may even
lead to grave scandal. Then, thanks to the diplomacy of
Mme de la Guichardie, again it appears that Gaston
Romilly has known the truth for years and that he also
has remained silent because his instinct wisely has
prompted him to keep the secret.

Life after all is a tangled skein, and if people in-
sisted on having everything clarified or exposed, un-
bearable situations would often come to light. The best
course is to say nothing—to pretend that nobody
knows—though it is tacitly understood that everybody
does know. This is not because people are generally

philosophers but because they are cowards. Nevertheless their instinct is fundamentally sound, for it is this
conspiracy of silence that makes life in common possible.

Personal recollections play an important part in most
of the novels cited, giving them the ring of at least
emotional sincerity. Yet Maurois never indulges in
outbursts of unbounded passion or unbridled expression; he always keeps within the bounds of restraint be-
fitting a gentleman. This personal element is much
more marked in his earlier works of fiction than in the
later. His first novels were for the most part mere literary transpositions of private adventures. The later
stories are composed to a large extent of material culled
from direct observation or else taken from the lives and
adventures of other people. Thus an important element
of interest, the reflection of his actual life, gradually
dwindles as time goes on.

On the other hand, and conversely, Maurois' novels
show a distinct trend from simplicity to complexity.
The earliest novels were somewhat bare and sketchy,
reduced by a process of simplification almost to a mere
outline. Later, he added observations, reflections, ideas,
more and more as occasion offered. His books become
overloaded with digressions, analyses of complicated
moral problems, their repercussions, and their psychological consequences. They grow richer in texture and
more weighty in thought and thus give more fitting
expression to the complex reality of the moral world.

Practically all Maurois' novels have the same setting.
Their general background is what might be called
French provincial upper middle-class life. This is the
stratum of society to which Maurois himself originally
belonged. It is made up of small manufacturers,
prominent merchants, and successful professional men;

occasionally, but not often, a landowner may be associated with the group. All are moderately wealthy—
sometimes much wealthier than the assessor of taxes is
led to believe!—but they live in a modest way. They
work hard; they have little imagination, but they possess a good deal of common sense and also a sense of
duty, or at least some vigorous prejudices—which in
their case are equally efficacious for practical purposes.
They appear to have very few vices; usually their failings are carefully concealed under a general cloak of
hypocrisy; but any tendencies toward irregularity are
for the most part repressed—crushed by the weight of
public opinion and by the fear of scandal. Hence count-
less little intrigues or individual upsets may be secretly
taking place beneath an austere show of outward respectability. A strong and sturdy people, prudent and
conservative, stern, reserved, and stolid, they form the
backbone of French provincial life. Maurois studied in
particular the type which flourishes in Normandy, and
which is perhaps more cautious, more greedy, and more
materialistic than the same class in other provinces; but
he never goes so far as to caricature a race which, with
all its faults, he respects for its fundamental qualities
and strength.

On the border line of this class, as it is pictured in
Maurois' books, are to be found a few sketches of the
provincial aristocracy. Aloof and touchy these people
are, for they have seen better days; but occasionally
there emerges from them a character of interest—a
perfect gentleman, an elderly rake, a volcanic young
woman, or some irrepressible dowager.

Parisian society is another field of Maurois' experience and the second important element in his books.
He is obviously not so much at ease in this environment

as in his own provincial circle. One feels that he is not completely at home in Paris. The provincial in him does not altogether approve of the exaggerated freedom of Parisian manners. What is more, he does not seem able to apprehend its secret charm, or at least he does not make it apparent to the reader. He seems to be struck mainly by external features; he makes a delightful and humorous sketch of the mannerisms of some hostess, or describes the dizzy course of brilliant and witty conversation in a fashionable *salon*, or again introduces us behind the scenes to view the arrangements, plots, and counterplots that are the prelude to some big event, such as a reception or some other function. His picture is always accurate and generally amusing but is to some extent superficial, and reflects after all the viewpoint of an outsider.

These various *milieux* are not represented by Maurois in a condition of static immobility. For Maurois is well aware that during the period covered by the majority of his novels (1900–1935) a profound transformation has occurred within the framework of French *bourgeois* society. At the beginning of the twentieth century, notwithstanding a few signs of incipient disintegration, the French social order seemed firmly rooted in a well-balanced though narrow traditionalism. The upheaval of the World War rocked the whole structure to its foundations. It accelerated the changes hitherto almost imperceptible, resulting in a wholesale abandonment of accepted conventions and the adoption of entirely new modes of existence. The new tendencies have not yet set in a definite trend; however, in their present state of flux it is easy to perceive a general loosening of all ties, links, and obligations, whether in the family circle, in the fields of personal morality, of

international law, or of business and professional eth-
ical standards. The changes have been so deep and so
rapid that now two generations stand side by side, not
only separated by the normal misunderstandings which
always crop up between fathers and sons but fundamentally opposed in their outlook as if they had come
to life in two entirely different epochs.

All Maurois' work as a novelist bears witness to this
conflict of the two generations. The older, with its roots
in the conventions and traditions of the past, is represented by a group of elderly couples and individuals all
displaying the same general characteristics. They are
all actively busy, sturdy, reliable; they conceal from
others their weaknesses and failings; from their behavior one may infer that they consider hypocrisy the
best social cement, and suppression and silence the sur-
est safeguards against catastrophe. In spite of their sur
face hardness—or perhaps because of it—they remain
at heart strangely sentimental, inclined to tinge the
realities of life with the fanciful colors of their imagination. The younger set is portrayed by Maurois as
much more direct, open, and frank. Their prejudices
are few; they show a lack of hypocrisy sometimes bor-
dering on impertinent and challenging cynicism. Many
of them entertain little respect for the older conventional standards of morality. Somewhat unreliable and
vacillating, they seem less constant than their elders in
their staying power. Yet they appear more vital and
spontaneous in their unabashed acceptance of everyday
life uncolored by the artificial hues of an outmoded
romanticism.

It is noteworthy that in Maurois' books, while the
older generation is generally presented against a provincial background, the younger set is often shown in a

Parisian environment. This fact stands in obvious relation to the successive stages of the writer's own experience: he was closely associated with the elderly types during his stay at Elbeuf; he became acquainted with the new, rising generation only after he himself had settled in the capital. Maurois does not dispense to one group or the other either praise or blame. Perhaps he has more confidence in the traditional conception of life as helping to make a comparative success of the haphazard business of existence; but he undoubtedly shows toward the aspirations of youth a constant, wholehearted sympathy and intelligent understanding.

Within the general framework of these surroundings, Maurois examines the two main problems of family life and modern business. To the traditional description of the old, powerful, and stuffy family atmosphere, so often met with in French literature, he adds very little that is unexpected and new. Maurois depicts essentially the type of family which was almost universal in prewar France and which is still predominant today in many of the provinces. It is the center around which every "good" man builds his life and ideals. The father has definite authority over his wife and children. The women are generally dependent and idle. The children's marriages are arranged by the parents or some matchmaker. When, for some reason or other, legitimate authority has been undermined or allowed to lapse, a crisis inevitably occurs. All members of the family group live in close proximity to one another, forming a strong and solid bulwark against adversity but at the same time mutually paralyzing any individual effort toward original development and autonomous expansion. In such an environment almost every form of affection may turn into a tyranny, and any trace of antagonism, after a period of repression, is bound to end in a violent explosion. But, whatever may happen, tradition and common sense unite to gather up the shattered fragments and weld them together once more, because French family life must go on.

Now and then, however, in Maurois' novels, and especially in the later ones, we can feel a storm of emancipation and revolt shaking the old, traditional edifice dangerously. In *Le Cercle de Famille* Denise is in open rebellion against the authority of her parents and schoolmasters; at an early age she takes the control of her life into her own hands; later her husband accepts with truly "modern" broad-mindedness the most elastic observance of marital ties. In *L'Instinct du Bonheur*, young Valentine and her fiancé have chosen each other without consulting their parents; it is noteworthy, however, that the moral obstacles to their marriage are smoothed out only through the wiles and intrigues of an old-fashioned matchmaker.

Maurois' description and evocation of the business world is more original and arresting. This subject has been frequently treated in French literature. Yet in most cases it is possible to discern the hand of the layman in some seemingly insignificant detail, and so the whole picture will fail to produce a convincing impression of reality. Maurois writes of things he knows well, and his descriptions ring true. He seldom offers an ambitious and exhaustive representation of industry or the channels of trade; but small technical details, generally unimportant in themselves though all obviously accurate, accompany the actions, words, and thoughts of the characters and create an atmosphere which one feels instinctively to be a true one.

The type of business most frequently pictured by

Maurois is one which is extremely common throughout France and with which Maurois himself was familiar during the early part of his career. As a rule it pivots upon an industrial establishment of moderate size and importance, in which the owner directs personally, sometimes jointly with another member of his family or with a trusted partner, all the operations connected with the purchasing of material and the production and sale of the finished article. An industrialist of this kind is naturally kept in close contact with his workmen, who to him are not an anonymous crowd but a group of actual human beings. Their instincts and prejudices he must be intimately aware of; according to circumstances he must be prepared to humor or restrain them, or to satisfy their demands. The firm is generally run on a modest and prudent scale. It may be affected to some extent by the great cycles of prosperity and depression; yet it possesses a degree of stability which is absent from more speculative, more impressive, and more adventurous undertakings. All these typical pictures are presented by Maurois in so definite and clear a manner that the daily life of the small provincial manufacturer and of the people revolving round him is conjured up before the reader's mind with great vividness and detail.

Now and again we catch a glimpse of business run on a grand scale, of big banks or other large concerns centered in Paris, with international ramifications spreading into foreign lands. With such vast enterprises Maurois had come in contact only sporadically. Consequently in his books "big business" always appears as a somewhat remote and mysterious entity, tremendously powerful in some respects—in others surprisingly weak and unstable. Here, instead of precise facts, we get hints and allusions only. Thus the reader's imagination is allowed to work and to envisage a dangerous monster, all the more disturbing in that it is vague and indefinite.

If we leave out of consideration a series of secondary characters, who are indeed fairly numerous but never play more than an episodical part in the development of the plot, the dramatis personae of Maurois' novels present a very limited and definite number of aspects. Thus for his men most of the characters seem to be partial variations of one central human type which bears a striking resemblance to the man Maurois himself. It is fairly easy to gather together the elements of this one type scattered throughout Maurois' novels and to form a synthetic picture of the original personage. He appears essentially as a *bourgeois*, the product of a comfortable home and solid family tradition. Intellectually refined and cultured, he is rather fond of theorizing and is inclined, especially in his youthful days, to set great store by abstract theories and systems. Strictly honest and conscientious on the one side, imaginative and broad-minded on the other, he suffers from a divided allegiance to these conflicting dispositions. Although capable of devoted yet jealous attachment in love, he is not an adept in the difficult art of dealing with women, perhaps because he is overcivilized, dangerously mistrustful, and at times morbidly self-analytical. In his latter days he finds contentment and peace in a silent understanding and philosophical acceptance of all the mediocrities of existence.

The various heroes of Maurois' novels sometimes embody one or another of the several opposing tendencies which coexisted in the original type but were divided up and developed independently in those fictitious characters for the sake of a clearer *exposé*; this is true, for instance, in the case of the two complementary figures in *Bernard Quesnay*—Antoine and Bernard, who represent, respectively, eagerness for life and dutiful submission to a dull, traditional routine. More often the characters of the novels simply correspond to successive periods in the development of the same coherent personality: thus Philippe Viniès does not go beyond the stage of the cocksure, theorizing youth; Philippe Marcenat, in early manhood, finds himself entangled in the inevitable complications of love; Bertrand Schmitt serves to illustrate the wise resignation which is the lot of a settled, mature age. At first sight these fictitious characters all appear to differ profoundly from one another, but they are in fact only complementary aspects and phases of the same psychological unity.

Maurois' women do not reflect the same fundamental unity of origin as the men. In fact they seem to be derived from two quite distinct sources—two types which must have hovered persistently in Maurois' imagination over a long period of years.

The most striking of these is perhaps the vital and glamorous young woman who appears, with many individual variations, as Odile in *Climats*, as Denise in *Le Cercle de Famille*, and to some extent as Simone and Françoise in *Bernard Quesnay*. She represents gaiety, art, intelligence, in contrast to the man, her opposite, who too often is absorbed in the dull routine of his work. She has beauty, brilliance, culture, and charm; she will respond to life with all the ardor of her temperamental nature. Self-centered and even selfish, she does not meekly submit to the rules of convention or to the pressure of circumstances. If thwarted or op-

posed in her desires she rebels and fights recklessly—
often without realizing the future consequences of her
actions—generally foredoomed, so at least hints Maurois, to come to dismal failure in the end. So Odile's
life ends in catastrophe; Denise is saved only by complete capitulation on the brink of a similar fate.

Sharply contrasting with these captivating and dangerous creatures are women like Isabelle in *Climats*
and Valentine in *L'Instinct du Bonheur*—models of the
willing slave demanding nothing from life but the privi-
lege of serving the man she loves. Modest and unassuming, they will accept even questionable compromises in
order to retain that love which makes their whole existence worth while. However, no really selfish motives
determine their behavior; they hardly think of themselves; they find happiness only in self-sacrifice. One
may wonder whether such a woman is ever to be found
in real life or whether she does not simply correspond to
an ideal image of the fairly common "clinging vine"
type—as seen through the eyes of the protective male,
longing for absolute and disinterested devotion. But
whatever the origin—real or half-imaginary—of this
conception of womanhood, Maurois obviously thinks
that this is the kind of woman who has the best chance
of finding the success and contentment which her more
vital and independent sister tries forcibly to secure and
usually fails to achieve.

Maurois' remaining novels do not offer either the
same elaborateness of structure or the same subtlety of
psychological analysis; they hardly ever contain any
noticeable touches of personal emotion. However, by
virtue of fantastic imagination combined with philosophical humor they do have a very distinctive interest.

Thus, in *Voyage au Pays des Articoles*, Maurois

imagines that a young Frenchman, Pierre Chambrelan, thoroughly disgusted with the atmosphere of postwar Europe, sets out for the South Seas in a small cutter with only a woman companion. As the tiny craft is blown off its course by a violent hurricane, he eventually lands on a small island inhabited by people of the most remarkable kind. The *élite* of this society is formed by a group of painters, sculptors, poets, and novelists who have devoted their whole lives to the exclusive cult of art. These few chosen "Articoles" are kept in comfort and relieved of any material worry or care by the mass of the "Beos"—short for "Beotians"—who cannot conceive of any higher honor or any greater delight than to provide food and entertainment for their illustrious yet useless artistic parasites. Indeed the "Articoles," being exempt from the wholesome struggle for existence, thanks to the worshipful admiration of the "Beos," are virtually cut off from the sane and normal world of reality, indulging in all sorts of extravagant and absurd imaginings. Pierre Chambrelan and his companion, though they are treated with much kindness and courtesy while they are waiting to resume their voyage, often have the eerie feeling that they are in the hands of people who are slightly but incurably insane.

In the fanciful picture of this imaginary island it is easy to discern a thinly veiled satire on certain exclusive literary circles to be found and even to be identified in Paris itself. Maurois, however, is too considerate and too well bred to write a satire with the pungency and caustic vigor of a Swift. His attacks are presented in so moderate and urbane a spirit that even his most pointed allusions are rendered innocuous. Yet even though his criticisms may be lacking in polemic force, the entertaining story brings forth with unusual clearness the fundamental idea that art deprived of contact with nature and reality is naught but folly.

Le Peseur d'Ames concerns an English doctor who indulges in gruesome experimentations on corpses taken to the postmortem department of the London hospital to which he is attached. Eventually he devises a method of collecting in especially constructed glass containers the "vital fluid" which is supposed to leave the body a few hours after death. The reason why he has chosen this strange field of study is that he is desperately in love with a young actress doomed, as he knows, to die very soon. Himself prepared to die by his own hand when this occurs, he hopes to contrive some means of bringing about a complete spiritual union between her and himself after death. In the course of his most unorthodox researches, he had mixed together in the same container the "vital fluid" of two persons who had been utterly devoted to each other during their lifetime and had discovered that, when placed in a beam of ultraviolet light, this mixture of "souls" took on an extraordinarily beautiful effulgence, which he interpreted as an indication and proof of absolute happiness. When the young woman he loves dies, the doctor immediately commits suicide. In anticipation of this event he had left with a trusted friend full instructions how to perform the necessary operations to ensure the preservation and fusion of their two "souls." But, alas, this friend, who has gone unexpectedly on a long journey, arrives too late and so ruins the doctor's carefully laid plans for attaining ineffable bliss through perfect union in love.

Such seems to be the meaning and purport of this grim little tale: In spite of all human hopes, anticipations, or strivings, the pursuit of absolute happiness through a complete spiritual conjunction with one we love is bound to end in failure in this world as well as beyond the grave.

In *La Machine à Lire les Pensées* the scene is laid in a much more cheerful environment and implies a less gloomy and despondent outlook upon existence. Maurois supposes that a French professor, M. Dumoulin, is asked to come to America and lecture for a few months at the fictitious University of Westmouth, very much as Maurois himself had been invited to lecture at Princeton. The account of M. Dumoulin's impressions and experiences in the United States is the pretext for a somewhat satirical, though on the whole very kindly and sympathetic, picture of American university life. At Westmouth, M. Dumoulin becomes especially well acquainted with one of his colleagues — Professor Hickey, a physicist. Hickey has just perfected a machine capable of recording every passing thought, even the most intimate, of a given person, without his or her knowledge. M. Dumoulin tries the machine on his own wife and discovers that she is very much occupied with recollections of a young cousin of hers with whom she had been friendly before her marriage and whom she mentally compares with her husband. It goes without saying that the comparison is not in the husband's favor. A quarrel ensues. Then Mme Dumoulin in her turn makes use of the "psychograph," as Professor Hickey calls his machine, and she finds that her husband is almost too appreciative of the charms of a lively young woman in one of his classes. Another quarrel results. However, we are told that the family atmosphere is now happier than before, as it has been cleared of unexpressed thoughts which had formerly been secretly poisoning it.

Professor Hickey eventually decides to place his invention on the market. The machine, however, is far from having the success he anticipated. In fact, it is soon discovered that the thoughts recorded by the "psychograph" do not represent any truly fundamental elements of human personality—and herein lies the philosophical idea that Maurois intended to convey in writing this complex little book.

According to him, the fugitive, indefinite ideas which at any given moment are passing through our mind are not truly expressive of our real inner nature. Just as the froth which sometimes rises to the surface of certain liquids in fermentation is not identical with the liquid itself, similarly from the depths of our consciousness arise more or less impure cravings, at times grandiose suggestions, which have no permanent place within our intimate normal selves and ought to be eliminated. These are thrown off in the form of obscure ideas, vague imaginings, fanciful daydreams which are not indeed the reflection of our true consciousness; it would be more exact to say that they are made up of things our personality has to eject. Our real personality expresses itself through clear concepts and definite actions.

The interest of such a theory is obvious. Many modern psychologists—and in particular those who advocate the methods of psychoanalysis—believe that our half-conscious thoughts and longings represent the most original and genuine part of our mental life. Maurois on the contrary affirms that they constitute only "one complementary side of the human being,"[5] and do not reveal anything of special interest concerning his real nature. The great defect of the "psychograph" was that through it the clear ideas which are the essentials

<hr/>

[5] A. Maurois, *La Machine à Lire les Pensées*, Nouvelle Revue Française, Paris, 1937, p. 196.

of our moral life were put on exactly the same plane
with elusive gusts of fancy which are only subsidiary
expressions of our being, often incompatible with its
true essence, and so the former were rendered absolutely indistinguishable from the latter. Thus the psychograph only stirred up confusion instead of promot-
ing clarity, and Maurois obviously intends to direct this
criticism against the school of psychology that this ap-
paratus stands for. According to Maurois, if we could
read *all* the thoughts of a man we would form an entirely erroneous view of his personality; in fact, our
conception of his true character would be much less
exact than if we had just examined objectively the purport and bearing of his voluntary actions. That is why
the thought-reading machine, as we are told at the end
of the story, very soon fell out of favor—and so probably will pass certain modern psychological theories—
after causing "much ado about nothing."[6]

Maurois' novels of the fantastic type are closely related to the *genre* of the philosophical tale after the
manner of Voltaire. They aim much less at studying
human character and manners than at illustrating some
abstract idea by means of entirely imaginary episodes
and circumstances. The starting point of the demon-
stration is some fanciful hypothesis, such as the organization of the island of the "Articoles," the possibility
of collecting a "vital fluid" in glass containers, or the
invention of an indiscreet and thoroughly efficient "psychograph." But, once the hypothesis is made, its implications and consequences are followed out with such
rigorous logic and such a subtle sense of natural human
reactions that at the end the reader finds himself accept-
ing the most incredible premises and, further, being led

[6] *La Machine à Lire les Pensées,* p. 217.

irresistibly to undeniable conclusions. With great cleverness Maurois takes care to place his extraordinary pieces of fiction in settings strange to the French reader, as a too familiar environment would make an overbold hypothesis look simply preposterous. Therefore he selects as the habitat of his "Articoles" a far-off island in the South Seas; he surrounds his "weigher of souls" with the mysterious atmosphere of the experimental laboratory of a London hospital; and the thought-reading machine comes into being in remote and bewildering America.

Moreover, the tale of entertaining and picturesque adventures in these strange places provides an element of exoticism which makes it easier for the reader to assimilate the earnest consideration of austere philosophical ideas. Here, however, the philosophical ideas are obviously the essential thing; the increasingly great importance they assume in the development of Maurois' works bears witness to the fundamental tendencies of his mind and talent.

5

MAUROIS'
PHILOSOPHY OF LIFE

ALL THE works of Maurois reflect a thoroughly
personal outlook on life. This implies not simply
the more or less original perception that every artist
must have of the colorful pageant of reality but a more
general, organized conception of the world as a whole—
in a word, a philosophy. Maurois is a philosopher by
deep, natural instinct. Chartier by his teaching seems
to have helped in no small degree to shape his spontaneous tendencies into a definite and positive system. As
time passed, the experiences of a life crowded with emotions and adventures had the effect of softening what
had perhaps been too rigid in Maurois' early theories,
and still more so of filling in the framework of his abstract ideas with a rich human substance. It is possible
to follow the development of his thought from his first
meager, sketchy books to the mellow maturity of his
later philosophical essays. Yet there has been no radical
change in the course of his moral evolution—merely a
continuous, harmonious, and regular growth.

The two essential questions on which the line of his
thoughts and speculations seems to have run are those of
action and of love. Both confronted him with particularly trying implications throughout a large part of his
life; both are repeatedly examined under one aspect or
another in practically every one of his works.

In his eyes no man can attain contentment and lasting

happiness unless he is able to accomplish something worth while in the field of concrete reality. Now creative action, he found, almost inevitably implies endless struggles, obscure and monotonous efforts, and, above all, sacrifice of those fanciful, artistic, and spiritual aspects of existence which constitute perhaps the main charm of life. Even when success comes at last as a well-deserved reward—as, for instance, in the case of Disraeli—it usually comes late, when the capacity for enjoyment is nearly exhausted, so that one may wonder if the palm is worth the duet after all. Again, there are those whose lives, like Bernard Quesnay's, are to the end just taken up with meaningless and mechanical routine. Yet without creative activity life is mere empty agitation, or even—as for the symbolic "Articoles"—sheer folly. Then the exercise of even the highest and noblest faculties of man degenerates into a dangerous or absurd game. So man finds himself hopelessly caught on the horns of a dilemma: to indulge in action means the abandonment of all that makes life beautiful and precious for the sake of an achievement that is often disappointing; to refrain from action means restlessness and discontent, as nowhere except in objective creation can man find self-realization, fulfillment, and balance.

Love, according to Maurois, holds prospects hardly less disheartening. Maurois had long nurtured the dream of a perfect union based on mutual respect and trust, growing richer in sympathy and devotion, and culminating in admirative worship. Yet he found that the gratification of such a longing is somehow denied to one and all. Reality always contrives to disintegrate romance. In *Byron*, in *Climats*, in *Le Peseur d'Ames*, in *Le Cercle de Famille*, and in *L'Instinct du Bonheur*, Maurois tirelessly and sometimes with a throb of almost

lyric emotion evokes the picture of the perennial, irrepressible quest of the human heart for perfect love. But
in every case either a catastrophe or resignation to inevitable disappointment is in store for the lover.

But is not action the essential element in a man's
practical existence, as love is the main factor in his inner
life? What if in both domains we have to meet with
irreducible contradictions, with insuperable antagonisms?
Maurois for his own part does not attempt to suggest
any new solution for these apparently insoluble problems. In the course of his own life he had in either case
to accept an imperfect compromise. What Maurois
wants to advocate is merely an attitude of mind and a
code of behavior which will enable us to live as con-
tentedly as possible while leaving unanswered the eternal questions for which no sage has yet found the solution.

The fundamental reason of man's failure to find an
absolute answer to the essential problems of action and
love is that, according to Maurois, an "absolute" of any
kind is completely beyond the reach of man. Maurois
is decidedly a relativist. In his opinion man is the measure of everything we know. He does not think that it
is possible to attain total, absolute truth in any field.
"Truth," commonly and conveniently so called, Maurois holds to be the view obtained when life is considered from one certain angle only. Truth varies
according to the observer and the slant of his vision.
It varies too in the individual in accordance with his
physical or mental condition. Even our most objective
opinions are as a rule determined subconsciously by
some deep instinctive repulsion or desire. Dr. O'Grady
speaks[1] of a country gentleman who, after comporting

[1] *Les Silences du Colonel Bramble*, pp. 190–91.

himself for many years as a good churchman, suddenly turned atheist. He was able to give very sound reasons for the change in his convictions, and would discuss points of doctrine with a great display of intelligence and learning; but the real reason of his loss of faith was that his wife had run away with a clergyman. Every man constructs for himself a more or less original ideology concerning the people and things he sees. In every case, however, his ideas are essentially the outcome, not of the actual facts to which they are supposed to apply, but of the deep instincts in the individual or even merely his passing moods. If there are conflicts of opinion, it is because different individuals view the same reality under the influence of different moods. "When one government says a thing is white and another that it is black, it is childish to think that one is right and the other wrong. France and England are both right, but their points of view are not the same and their respective truths are contradictory."[2] The trouble is that people are all determined to stand by their own particular conception of the world. Individuals, groups, nations are, each and every one of them, locked up, as it were, in a "private universe"[3] of their own conceiving, which for them constitutes the only possible basis of truth.

The only place in which an "absolute" can be attained is the world of illusion, which in one of his works Maurois calls "Meïpe." "Meïpe" is the name which little Françoise—who obviously represents Michelle, André Maurois' young daughter—had given to the "never never land" of her childish dreams. " 'Meïpe' is the name of a town, a country, a universe, perhaps,

[2] *Les Discours du Docteur O'Grady*, p. 252.
[3] *Mes Songes que voici*, pp. 16–21.

which she has invented. There she takes refuge whenever the external world becomes hostile to her. . . . .
On days when Françoise has had to go without dessert,
the pastry-cooks of 'Meïpe' standing at the door of
their shops distribute cakes to the passers-by. On eve-
nings when Françoise has been crying, 'Meïpe,' seen
through her tears with its thousand glittering lights, is
even more beautiful than on other days."[4]

According to Maurois, not only little children but
nearly all adults too at one time or another seek shelter
from the hard facts of reality in a marvelous imaginary
world. The artist creates a world of his own to compensate for his private misfortunes. The more unhappy he
may be in actual life, the richer in emotions will be the
world of his creation. *"Presque toutes les vies sont
ratées, Monsieur Schmitt, et c'est pourquoi vous autres
écrivains vous formez des destins imaginaires,"*[5] says
a wise *Abbé* in *Le Cercle de Famille*. Religious feelings in the same way feed and thrive on personal disappointments and suffering. "You have no right to be
happy, Monsieur Schmitt. Religion and art need unhappiness."[6] Business, especially on a large scale, is for
many a man a fantastic realm wherein imagination can
have free play. Money is after all but a minor pawn in
the game. The main advantage of work in most cases
is that it enables a man to forget some unpleasant fact
in everyday reality. Why did Holmann get involved
in big enterprises? His matrimonial life was a failure
and so "he lost himself in business, as an unhappy play-
wright escapes into his drama or a novelist into his

---

[4] A. Maurois, *Meïpe*, Grasset, Paris, 1926, p. xi.
[5] A. Maurois, *Le Cercle de Famille*, Grasset, Paris, 1932, p. 272.
[6] *Ibid.*, p. 274.

novel."[7] War itself, says Maurois,[8] is accepted by all—
loved even by some—in spite of its atrocities, because
it takes people out of themselves, away from their humdrum existence and the wearying problems of everyday
life. It transports them into an unreal world which is
like a dream—a bad dream of mud and blood—but a
dream nevertheless.

Two deep human yearnings are conjoined in
"Meïpe"—first, the desire to escape from real life
with its monotonous struggle and its thankless tasks;
second, the longing to be delivered from the thwarted
aspirations with which the soul has been encumbered.
That explains why Maurois gave his book the title of
Meïpe ou la Delivrance, and why "Meïpe" holds the
key to happiness. "One after another our friends discover the mysterious kingdom of Françoise, and more
than one, when he thinks of happiness, no longer hopes
to find it anywhere but in 'Meïpe'."[9]

It must not be thought that this world of illusion
is entirely distinct from the world we live in. The two
are interdependent. Illusion feeds on life, and life
feeds on illusion. On the one hand, actual facts are the
raw material of fiction. The artist who transposes his
sufferings into an imaginative creation has his own experience for a foundation; daydreams are based on
fragments of things seen or heard; the business man
with "vision" has to take facts into account as well;
and if war seems to us a nightmare, it is also a stern
reality. On the other hand, reality is shot through
with dreams: people try to make their dreams come
true; they shape their conduct according to imaginary

[7] Ibid., p. 267.

[8] Les Silences du Colonel Bramble, pp. 75–77.

[9] Meïpe, p. xii.

models often taken directly from works of fiction, and such illusory examples may have a tremendous influence on their destiny. In one of the short stories[10] illustrating this side of his theory about "Meïpe," Maurois tells of a young man, Lecadieu, who is a brilliant scholar, dashing and ambitious, outwardly rather cynical, though really romantic at heart, and a great reader of Balzac. Being *léger d'argent,* he accepts a post as a tutor to the sons of an influential politician, Trélivan. Trélivan's wife is pretty, neglected, and bored. Lecadieu begins courting her persistently, risks a declaration—and is requested to leave. On his way out, however, he remembers a story by Balzac in which a young man, after being dismissed in similar circumstances, returns immediately under a pretext and carries his point. So Lecadieu, conforming his behavior to the example of the novel, also finds a pretext; and, as in the meantime Mme Trélivan has apparently regretted her excess of virtue, he becomes her lover. Trélivan is soon aware of the state of affairs; and as he himself wants to get rid of his wife in order to marry a young actress, he manages to obtain proofs of the liaison. He then has a very gentlemanly interview with Lecadieu in which he makes certain stipulations. He wants a divorce, but no scandal. Lecadieu will obtain an appointment as a schoolteacher in a remote provincial town. Trélivan promises to arrange the matter, even to the point of securing him promotion, and he is as good as his word. But years pass, and the once-ambitious Lecadieu, who has married Mme Trélivan, a woman twelve years his senior, is still a poor, shabbily dressed schoolteacher—and it is all M. de Balzac's fault!

It is indeed necessary that there should be constant

---

[10] "Par la faute de M. de Balzac," *Meïpe.*

intercourse between the world of reality and the imaginary realm of "Meïpe." One without the other is incomplete and ineffectual. On the one hand, the real without the ideal is dull and drab. Bernard Quesnay succeeded in expunging all dreams from his life and thus became a mere automaton, with no other purpose but to run a factory and to manufacture cloth. On the other hand, if the world of the imagination fails to keep in touch with reality, as in *Le Pays des Articoles*, the result is empty, useless, and senseless extravaganza.

In fact only very exceptionally does a man achieve a happy blending of the world of reality and the world of illusion. Generally the hard facts or the volatile dreams alternately take the upper hand, according to circumstances; and a man will swing back and forth from reality to "Meïpe" and from "Meïpe" to reality. But with each swing of the pendulum he encounters a thousand possibilities of self-fulfillment. A static equilibrium is very nearly impossible and could never be permanent. A happy balance cannot be reached at a fixed intermediate position between two extreme points, but a series of oscillations may give both "Meïpe" and reality a fair chance of development within the human mind, while continual new adjustments are necessary in order to correct exaggerations or compensate for deficiencies in one field or another.

An unstable equilibrium of a similar order may be the explanation of the oft-discussed problem of man's dual nature. In conjunction with the generous, altruistic, idealistic being that exists to some extent in every one of us and which is the side of our nature we like to exhibit to the world, there is also a nasty, brutish, selfish animal concealed in the depths of every human soul. According to Maurois, the brutish animal seems to be a survival within us of the original primitive man,[11] and the moral being in us is a product of society and civilization. Man was gradually constrained by the necessities of life in the society of his kind to adopt altruistic attitudes by no means spontaneous in him. The wild animal that he was at first was tamed down and made gentler under pressure of the group—the "pack"—to which he belonged: "The pack has made good citizens out of us. We have a conscience, which is the instinct of stupidly carrying out, for the good of the herd, actions that are dangerous to the individual. We experience remorse, a painful sensation of having deserved the contempt of the horde, and we write books on morals in order to prove that the customs adopted by the majority of the wolves are derived from eternal principles."[12]

Whatever their origin, the two tendencies mentioned above are present in man and both must be satisfied. If one of the two is sacrificed for the benefit of the other, trouble is bound to follow. Sometimes civilization in the form of education, family influence, or moral pressure exerted by environment tries to stamp out of existence the primitive man, the sly, greedy, sensual, immoral beast that lies more or less dormant in ourselves. As a rule such attempts have succeeded only in awakening the brute and goading him to revolt. Maurois quotes[13] as examples the cases of Gide and Byron. The rebel then throws off all ties and conventions and expects to find happiness in the complete satisfaction of his elementary instincts—in other words,

[11] *Mes Songes que voici*, p. 47.
[12] *Les Discours du Docteur O'Grady*, pp. 52–53.
[13] *Mes Songes que voici*, p. 40.

in freedom. Almost inevitably he finds that happiness
eludes him. Though he be entirely free, he remains
dissatisfied, restless. He is completely at a loss to know
why it should be so. The reason is that he has gone to
the other extreme and the civilized man in him suffers
and protests. Man has been part of a society so long
that, just as it was impossible for society to eradicate
from man all traces of the primitive animal, in the
same way it is impossible for man to abolish in himself
the stamp put upon him by uncounted generations of
civilized ancestors. That is partly why women, on having attained complete emancipation, have not found
that it brings them the happiness they expected.[14] That
is why Byron, having cast aside all accepted standards
of morality, found himself, though free, still more unhappy than before. Unbeknown to himself, the best
part of him, the civilized man that was in him, was
clamoring for restraint and the conventions.

Conventions are not very popular nowadays. Maurois comes forward as their champion and proclaims
them necessary, just, and good. For him the only way
to face this disappointing and disharmonious world of
ours, with a measure of confidence and a chance of success, is to import into it elements of organization and
order which do not—or did not originally—belong
there. Conventions, as he understands them, are all
the rules of conduct which are not part of man's primitive nature but which have been imposed on him by the
implications of life in society with other men. They
are the tacit or recognized agreements accepted and en-
forced by all civilized society for the good of the community and of the individual. There is a great variety
of them, and they are not all of the same age or of the

[14] *Ibid.*, p. 47.

same importance. Some are very old—so old indeed
that they are very deeply ingrained in us and in fact
may now be considered as an integral part of modern
human nature. Such are the fundamental "moral principles," relating, for instance, to marriage and sex. Any-
one who tries in one way or another to repudiate them—
as Byron did—will be torn within himself and will have
to endure great unhappiness. Some of the conventions,
being of more recent origin, are not definitely incor-
porated in human nature and yet, as a rule, are fairly
well established among the members of certain given
types of society. These are the obligations of common
morality pertaining to politics, trade, profession, property, and so on. To complete the list we have the most
recent, unstable, and superficial acquisitions, commonly
referred to as "social conventions," whose infringement
entails no worse penalty than a little scandal or the
suspicious frownings of a small, restricted group.

Maurois insists that no matter when they may have
come into existence they all have the same origin, the
same nature, and the same important function in our
lives; they are the link between the individual and his
social environment, and an individual cannot be happy
unless he is outwardly and inwardly in sympathy with
the prevailing "conventions" of the society in which
he is placed. They give his social life an intelligible
meaning and purpose. Man needs to believe in some
ideal—in patriotism, in justice, in democracy, in race,
or in some other abstraction—in order that he may accept more or less cheerfully the restraints imposed upon
him by society. Without such beliefs, such conventions,
such myths, life in the society of our fellow men would
be unlivable. Therefore they are man's most precious
possessions, though he is generally not even aware of it.

Indeed, they constitute for him a veritable "Trésor caché,"[15] a hidden treasure.

For Maurois' argument the actual origin of these conventions is of very little moment. In fact, some conventions, having a very problematical foundation or no foundation at all—being pure fictions—are at least as efficacious as the practical conventions which are based upon some obvious reality. Those conventions which have a limited contact with reality offer few loopholes for eventual criticism. The more mythical they are, the longer they will last. Since it is practically impossible to grasp and apprehend them, they appear correspondingly intangible. Yet no myth or convention is, properly speaking, eternal. Inevitably somebody discovers sooner or later that conventions are only conventions after all. When the generality of people in a given group become aware of the artificial nature of their common beliefs, a revolution takes place, and peace cannot be restored until a new set of conventions has been accepted by all.

Maurois in *Mes Songes que voici* gives a fanciful but illuminating example of the mechanism of convention. He imagines that a group of enterprising Englishmen have succeeded in reaching the moon, traveling in a rocket-shell. But for some reason they are unable to return to the earth. They prepare to remain permanently on the satellite. They set to work, manufacture synthetic foodstuffs, establish an oxygen factory, and of course organize a regular British crown colony with a solemn Resident Governor. For many generations these Englishmen in their new home continue to behave as if they were still in England. They dress for dinner every evening. The laws are promulgated

[15] *Mes Songes que voici*, p. 28.

in the name of the King of Great Britain and Ireland,
Emperor of India, Protector of the Moon. On the
King's birthday the colonists give the toast to His Maj-
esty "The King!" through their oxygen masks. Everybody is respectful and happy. But after a few centuries
have passed in uneventful and peaceful prosperity,
some iconoclastic Anglo-Lunaries begin to question the
terrestrial "legend." Why should British conventions
rule the activities of life in the Moon? Who is that
invisible King of England anyway? The lunar youth,
anxious to lead a freer life, eagerly adopt the revolutionary theories, and we are told that very soon afterward serious trouble spreads all over the surface of the
Moon. The Lunaries had lost the mainspring of their
energy, their belief in the sacrosanctity of British conventions, their faith in the remote and mythical King—
in a word, their hidden treasure.

Conventions are not to be regarded as eternal. Being
intermediary between the individual and his surroundings, they must be well adapted to both. Adequate
adaptation of conventions to men and their environment means order. When the environment changes,
the conventions must be altered to fit the new organization of things. Since environment is steadily changing practically all the time, conventions must be plastic
and evolve harmoniously or they collapse. That is the
basis of Maurois' reformist conservatism. In order to
retain the conventions, which are a good and necessary
legacy from the past, it is essential to keep them up to
date, to adapt them by incessant reforms to the ever
changing conditions of social surroundings. That is
what Disraeli was aiming at in politics. Continual
adaptation of conventions, of ideas, of principles to
perpetually changing facts is the condition and the

guaranty of order. Many people try to do the reverse; they attempt to adapt reality to principles, ideas, or conventions. This was the aim and object of Shelley and of the hero in *Ni Ange, ni Bête*, and also of Maurois himself when he was very young. Such people would be dangerous fools if they had any real power; but as a rule they fail dismally in their attempts before they can do any serious harm.

Environment is too complex to be shaped and molded by the will of man. Man is shaped and molded by pressure of his environment—often formed entirely by it. The process, however, is not as simple as is sometimes imagined. The influence is not always direct; quite frequently our actions are merely reactions against an aggressive world, acts of retaliation or compensation for some personal inferiority; but at all events the environment primarily conditions even that reaction. Moreover, reaction or retaliation is often of a temporary nature. Slowly and surely reality claims and tames the rebellious individual and obliges him to do the very thing against which he revolted: Bernard Quesnay runs the factory as his grandfather did before him. Denise, after fighting all her life against the example of her mother, ends in doing exactly what her mother did.

Can man then be considered as free? Theoretically, yes, says Maurois. "A man can change everything. A child would not have the strength to move a locomotive, yet he can set it going if he opens the right throttle."[16] But unless the child knows how the locomotive works, it will be the most amazing stroke of luck if he chances to turn the right lever. More likely than not he will never touch it at all. Now we have hardly any more knowledge of the forces governing the world at large

[16] *Les Discours du Docteur O'Grady*, p. 164.

than the child has of the locomotive, and so we cannot make those forces work according to our fancy.

Who has organized these forces and who makes them work? A wise and providential Divinity? Well, says Maurois, "I wish I could believe it . . . . , but I confess that if I look around me I do not see the effects of that benevolent wisdom. I see the wicked triumphant, the ambitious rewarded, murderers strongly established in power, the just stricken with terrible diseases. I see coquettes surrounded by submissive men, virtuous women disdained."[17] This world obviously is not a happy place. "Byron finds manifestations in the universe of the wilful activity of a cruel fate, hostile to man. I myself," adds Maurois, "perceive a universe, powerful and pitiless and at the same time indifferent to the individual."[18]

The standpoint reached by Maurois might be called a desperate optimism. "I like your optimism," says Denise to Bertrand Schmitt, who obviously stands for Maurois himself in *Le Cercle de Famille*, ". . . . it has a touch of desperation about it that pleases me."[19]

The causes of the despair are only too obvious. The crucial problems of life—those of action and love—seem hopelessly insoluble; the absolute, the ideal, which alone could bring perfect happiness, is unattainable; there is no real justice, no apparent Providence, no true, broad, practical freedom; mankind is no more than a "pitiful group of mammals,"[20] causing some stir for the nonce on this planet, but no more important in itself than an ant-hill.[21]

[17] *Mes Songes que voici*, p. 25. [18] *Ibid.*, pp. 19–20.
[19] *Le Cercle de Famille*, p. 323.
[20] *Les Silences du Colonel Bramble*, p. 46.
[21] *Mes Songes que voici*, pp. 33–36.

And yet this desperate condition of affairs can and must be faced with sincere optimism. The one sure way to escape from the petty and sordid contingencies of reality is through the marvelous world of illusion. "Meïpe," the world of illusion, offers a happy refuge to any dreamer who wishes to find shelter there. It is open to all people at all times now and forever. This same world of illusion also provides the myths, beliefs, and conventions that make life itself not only bearable but even interesting, pleasant, and truly worth living. It may be a saddening thought that our reasons for living are nothing but phantoms of the imagination, but it is also comforting to think that they are perhaps all the more beautiful on that account. Therefore we must abide by them. We must not try to upset them, because we know they are pure conventions. We must be continually adapting them to a changing reality, but only in order to keep them strong and firm. Revolt leads nowhere. The salvation of mankind lies in an intelligent conformism.

Conformism and intelligence are probably the two words which best summarize the fundamental characteristics of André Maurois. The root of his conformism is undoubtedly to be found in the powerful influence under which he came in his youth at Elbeuf. His sensitive nature had always been very receptive and susceptible to the "atmosphere"—or, as he himself said, to the "climate"—of people and places. He himself became thoroughly impregnated with the moral atmosphere of the good provincial *bourgeoisie* among whom he spent the early part of his life. He carried it with him more or less unconsciously wherever he went. That he could so easily understand and so aptly interpret the English to the French is perhaps because he found in

the English people a spirit which was in many respects
akin to that which prevailed in his own original environment just across the Channel and which is character-
ized by a certain lack of intellectual brilliancy and a
great respect for external convention, resting on a solid
foundation of modest and unassuming decency. That
background of common, simple morality he has retained
throughout his life. He has stubbornly adhered to his
faith in honesty, in sincerity, in the family. In a century fertile in audacious and questionable theories, he
has consistently fought on the side of the traditional
conceptions of marriage, friendship, industry, professional honesty. These respectable conceptions appear
in his books adapted to modern conditions of life, but
all quite recognizable in their new guise.

There is also in Maurois something which was not
part of his original surroundings—his intellectual capacity. In fact, it was his intellectual capacity that
caused the conflict with his environment and ultimately
tore him away from it. Chartier undoubtedly contributed greatly to the development of that aspect of his
pupil's personality, but the best explanation that can be
found for it is that it is a purely personal and exceptional gift. Above all Maurois is anxious to understand.
In him creative power is clearly subordinated to an in-
terpretative tendency. He does not paint a picture for
the sake of the subject—nor indeed even for the sake
of the picture—but rather for the purpose of portraying
a psychological mechanism. It is for this reason that his
work as a biographer is so outstanding. It is easier for
him to take a character to pieces than to create an original one. This is the quality that determined his great
life work of interpreting the English to the French.
His longing to understand goes hand in hand with an

extraordinary perspicacity and complete sincerity. Even
when it comes to examining the things which are dear-
est to him, he does not shrink from what he considers
to be the truth, however unpalatable that may be; so he
discovers that even his own moral ideas—and ideals—
are nothing but conventions. He has to admit this, and
does not hesitate to proclaim it. But since he considers
these ideals a necessary part of life, even though they
are conventions, he will retain them as conventions,
and indeed as illusions, if need be. It would be difficult
to find anywhere a more perfect example of fair-
mindedness and shrewdness combined. This combination is the key to Maurois' life and to his work, which
is his life.

Some conservative moral ideas which he has were
acquired from his original environment. An innate personal gift for intellectual criticism and creation turned
him from his traditional way of living and thinking.
For years he had to fight to establish a balance between
the two. He oscillated between these opposite poles,
and finally created a vigorous and yet comprehensive
unity in his life and in his doctrine. As Dr. O'Grady
says: *"Toute doctrine est une autobiographie."*[22]

[22] *Les Discours du Docteur O'Grady,* p. 174.

BIBLIOGRAPHY

I. WORKS BY ANDRÉ MAUROIS

Les Silences du Colonel Bramble. B. Grasset, Paris, 1918.

Ni Ange, ni Bête. B. Grasset, Paris, 1919.

Les Bourgeois de Witzheim. B. Grasset, Paris, 1920.

Les Discours du Docteur O'Grady. (Previously published under a slightly different form as *Le Général Bramble*, Grasset, 1918—limited edition.) B. Grasset, Paris, 1922.

Ariel ou la Vie de Shelley. (Previously published in *Les Cahiers Verts*, No. 22 [1923],) B Grasset, Paris, 1923.

Dialogues sur le Commandement. (Previously published in *Les Cahiers Verts*, No. 46 [1924].) B. Grasset, Paris, 1924.

Arabesques. Marcelle Lesage, Paris, 1925.

Les Anglais. Les Cahiers Libres, Toulouse, 1926.

Bernard Quesnay. (Previously published in a shorter form as "La Hausse et la Baisse" in *Les Œuvres Libres*, 1922.) Nouvelle Revue Française, Paris, 1926; revised and enlarged edition, 1928.

Meïpe ou la Délivrance. B. Grasset, Paris, 1926. (Reprinted as *Les Mondes Imaginaires*; same text with addition of "Les Derniers Jours de Pompeï," Grasset, 1929.)

La Vie de Disraëli. Nouvelle Revue Française, Paris, 1924.

Conseils à un jeune Français partant pour l'Angleterre. (Previously published in *Les Amis d'Edouard*, No. 118), Abbeville, 1927.

La Conversation. Hachette, Paris, 1927.

Petite Histoire de l'Espèce Humaine (fragments). Les Cahiers de Paris, Paris, 1927.

Un Essai sur Dickens. (Previously published in *Les Cahiers Verts*, 1927.) B. Grasset, Paris, 1927.

Études Anglaises. B. Grasset, Paris, 1927.

Le Chapitre suivant. Kra, Paris, 1927.

Rouen. Émile-Paul, Paris, 1927.

Aspects de la Biographie. Au Sans Pareil, Paris, 1928.

Voyage au Pays des Articoles. J. Schiffrin, Éditions de la Pléiade, Paris, 1928.

Climats. B. Grasset, Paris, 1928.

Contact. Stols, Paris, 1928.

Le Pays des trente-six mille Volontés. Le Coffret des Histoires Extraordinaires, Paris, 1928.

Fragments d'un Journal de Vacances. Emile Hazan, Paris, 1929.

Le Côté de Chelsea. (First published in *La Revue de Paris,* 1929.) Ed. du Trianon, Paris, 1929.

Don Juan ou la Vie de Byron. B. Grasset, Paris, 1930.

Relativisme. Kra, Paris, 1930.

Patapoufs et Filifers. Hartman, Paris, 1930.

Tourgueniev. (First published in *La Revue Hebdomadaire,* 1930.) B. Grasset, Paris, 1931.

Le Peseur d'Ames. Nouvelle Revue Française, Paris, 1931.

Sur le vif—L'Exposition coloniale de Paris, 1931. Degorce, Paris, 1931.

Lyautey. Plon, Paris, 1931.

L'Amérique inattendue. Éditions Mornay, Paris, 1931.

Voltaire. Peter Davies, London, 1932.

Proust et Ruskin. Oxford, 1932. (Essays and studies by members of the English Association.)

L'Anglaise et d'autres femmes. La Nouvelle Société d'Éditions, Paris, 1932.

Le Cercle de Famille. B. Grasset, Paris, 1932.

Mes Songes que voici. B. Grasset, Paris, 1933.

Introduction à la méthode de Paul Valéry. Les Cahiers Libres, Paris, 1933.

Edouard VII et son temps. Éditions de France, Paris, 1933.

Chantiers Américains. Nouvelle Revue Française, Paris, 1933.

L'Instinct du Bonheur. B. Grasset, Paris, 1934.

Sentiments et Coutumes. B. Grasset, Paris, 1934.

Magiciens et Logiciens. B. Grasset, Paris, 1935.

Histoire d'Angleterre. A. Fayard, Paris, 1937.
La Machine à Lire les Pensées. Nouvelle Revue Française, Paris, 1937.
Chateaubriand. B. Grasset, Paris, 1938.
Un Art de vivre. Plon, Paris, 1939.

II. ENGLISH TRANSLATIONS OF MAUROIS' WORKS

Les Silences du Colonel Bramble. Translated by Thurfride Wake and W. Jackson as *The Silence of Colonel Bramble,* John Lane, London and New York, 1919.
Le Général Bramble (first form of *Les Discours du Docteur O'Grady*). Translated by Jules Castier and Ronald Boswell as *General Bramble,* John Lane, London and New York, 1921.
Ariel ou la Vie de Shelley. Translated by Ella d'Arcy as *Ariel, a Shelley Romance,* John Lane, London, 1924; and as *Ariel, the Life of Shelley,* D. Appleton, New York, 1924.
Dialogues sur le Commandement. Translated by John Lewis May as *Captains and Kings; Three Dialogues on Leadership,* John Lane, London, 1925; D. Appleton, New York, 1925.
Meïpe ou la Délivrance. Translated by Eric Sutton as *Mape: the World of Illusion,* John Lane, London, 1926; D. Appleton, New York, 1926.
Bernard Quesnay. Translated by Brian W. Downs as *Bernard Quesnay,* Jonathan Cape, London, 1927; D. Appleton, New York, 1927.
La Vie de Disraëli. Translated by Hamish Miles as *Disraeli: a Picture of the Victorian Age,* John Lane, London, 1927; D. Appleton, New York, 1927.
Le Chapitre suivant. Translated as *The Next Chapter: the War against the Moon,* K. Paul, Trench, Trubner & Company, London, 1927; E. P. Dutton & Company, New York, 1927.

Aspects de la Biographie. Translated by S. C. Roberts as *Aspects of Biography*, Cambridge University Press, 1928; D. Appleton, New York, 1929.

Voyage au Pays des Articoles. Translated by David Garnett as *A Voyage to the Island of the Articoles*, Jonathan Cape, London, 1928; D. Appleton, New York, 1929.

Climats. Translated by Joseph Collins as *Whatever Gods May Be*, Cassell, London, 1929; and as *Atmosphere of Love*, D. Appleton, New York, 1929.

Don Juan ou la Vie de Byron. Translated by Hamish Miles as *Byron*, Jonathan Cape, London, 1930; D. Appleton, New York, 1930.

Le Côté de Chelsea. Translated by Hamish Miles as *Chelsea Way*, Mathews & Marrot, London, 1930.

La Conversation. Translated by Yvonne Dufour as *Conversation*, E. P. Dutton, New York, 1930.

Le Pays des trente-six mille Volontés. Translated by Pauline Fairbanks as *The Country of Thirty-six Thousand Wishes*, W. Heinemann, London, 1930; D. Appleton, New York, 1930.

Le Peseur d'Ames. Translated by Hamish Miles as *The Weigher of Souls*, Cassell, London, 1931; D. Appleton, London and New York, 1931.

Lyautey. Translated by Hamish Miles as *Marshal Lyautey*, John Lane, London, 1931; and as *Lyautey*, D. Appleton, New York, 1931.

Voltaire. Translated by Hamish Miles as *Voltaire*, P. Davies, London, 1932; D. Appleton, New York, 1932.

Le Cercle de Famille. Translated by Hamish Miles as *The Family Circle*, Cassell & Company, London, 1932; D. Appleton, New York, 1932.

Conseils à un jeune Française partant pour l'Angleterre; Le Côté de Chelsea; Mes Songes que voici; fragments of *L'Amérique inattendue* and *Chantiers Américains.* Translated by Hamish Miles as *A Private Universe*, D. Appleton, New York, 1932.

Edouard VII et son temps. Translated by Hamish Miles as
   King Edward and His Times, Cassell & Company, Lon-
   don, 1933; and as *The Edwardian Era,* D. Appleton,
   New York, 1933.

Essai sur Dickens. Translated by Hamish Miles as *Dickens,*
   Harper & Brothers, New York and London, 1935.

L'Anglaise et d'autres femmes. Translated by Hamish Miles
   as *Ricochets; Miniature Tales of Human Life,* Harper
   & Brothers, New York and London, 1935.

Magiciens et Logiciens. Translated by Hamish Miles as
   Prophets and Poets, Harper & Brothers, New York and
   London, 1935.

Histoire d'Angleterre. Translated by Hamish Miles as *The
   Miracle of England,* Harper & Brothers, New York and
   London, 1937.

La Machine à Lire les Pensées. Translated by James Whitall
   as *The Thought-Reading Machine,* Harper & Brothers,
   New York and London, 1938.

Chateaubriand. Translated by Vera Fraser as *Chateaubriand
   Poet, Statesman, Lover,* Harper & Brothers, New York
   and London, 1938.

INDEX

(The titles of books by André Maurois are indicated by an asterisk.)